May God bless you
Nadine Van Riper

Life's Journey With God

Through Laughter and Tears

by Nadine Van Riper

XULON PRESS

CONTENTS

ACKNOWLEDGMENTS

This book would not be complete without expressing our deepest gratitude to all who contributed to our work in the ministry in some way over the past 50 plus years.

God will surely bless all of you who prayed for our ministry over the years as we followed God's Will in our lives whether as traveling evangelists or in a pastorate.

Some individuals and families invited us into their homes, others supported our evangelistic mission financially, family and friends donated food and other goods when we were in dire need, and countless others prayed diligently for our safety in the states and abroad as well as for God's Will to work in the lives of those we ministered to along the way.

I am truly grateful to my beloved mother, Gernie Bennett, for realizing the importance and guiding my musical talents for the glory of our Lord.

Basil Bennett, my oldest brother, took it upon himself to buy my first piano, for which I am forever grateful. It was the beginning of a long career playing gospel music.

Dolores Barnett, my sister and eldest sibling, deserves much gratitude for doing some of my everyday chores while I diligently practiced playing the piano every evening while we were children. From a young age, my musical talent was used in church services. God has surely blessed Dolores for her selflessness and cheerful demeanor.

I'm grateful for the cover photo taken by George late one summer evening when we noticed an incredible sunset silhouetting the cross with beautiful colors gracing the sky and had to capture the moment. The cross is made with telephone poles and installed four feet deep in the ground anchored with concrete against strong winds on the hilltop. The stipe (vertical post) stands almost 35-foot tall with an 8-foot patibulum (cross-arm). We once adorned it with a wreath of thorns that stayed there for a couple years. We placed the cross there as a symbol of Christ's love for humanity and wanted people traveling Route 40 to also be able to view it. Maybe someday we will have it lit at night.

And finally, George and I especially extend our gratefulness to our niece, Teresa Crerand (Dolores' daughter), for her dedication in setting aside many hours to edit this book and prepare it for publication. Some of her photographs are also included in this book. As we worked together, we shared laughter where family humor comes to life on these pages, but also tears over family tragedies and losses. I truly believe without Teresa's professional expertise in journalism, this book would have never been published. An added advantage for me was that she knows so much of our family history and with her guidance this book came to fruition.

It is my hope that you will benefit somehow from reading about my family and relate to the many experiences we encountered, some joyful, some painful, but also some laughter in lighter moments.

Nadine Van Riper

INTRODUCTION

Our story begins in a small town in southern West Virginia where I was born the youngest of five children into a musically talented family. My mother could play any stringed instrument with astonishing skill, all self-taught. While she mostly played the violin and guitar over the years, her favorite instrument was the banjo. My father was also musically gifted and together they formed a group with him playing the banjo.

At six weeks of age, I nearly lost my life but God spared it. His plan unfolds in these pages as He molded my musical gift and love of playing the piano beginning in my childhood years, and prepared me for life as a minister's wife and the journey to come, all according to God's plan.

As servants of God, we overcame many obstacles and challenges during more than 50 years in the ministry in pastorates and as traveling evangelists. In obedience to God's Will, we impacted the lives of others worldwide, reached many with our music ministry, including our radio ministry now continued through our retirement years.

We raised three fine sons along the way who grew into hand-some intelligent young men and also yielded to the call of our Lord. Over the years, we shared wonderful as well as heartbreaking times together. When we lost one, it changed our lives forever. Truly, we serve God through laughter and tears as we fulfill His plan for our lives. I hope you enjoy reading these pages about one of God's families and are inspired along the way!

DEDICATION

This book is dedicated to my wonderful and loving husband, George, who has been so supportive and encouraging as I spent numerous hours penning the many thoughts and memories that are very near and dear to my heart. I also dedicate it to our three sons, Nevin, the eldest, Scot, the youngest, both of whom we deeply cherish, and in memory of our middle son, Craig, whom we miss more than words can express and look forward to a wonderful reunion in heaven.

Chapter 1

My Beginning In West Virginia

L et me set the scene for you in a small southern town just prior to my birth into a musically gifted family. After the cold harsh winds of a 1937 winter ceased, spring was on the horizon as winter's last blanket of snow finally melted away. Dark and barren trees awakened from a long winter's nap, sap began to flow, and leaves made their appearance.

Once again, Mother Nature displayed beautiful shades of green all over the hillsides. It was such a gorgeous sight to behold when flowers joined in with their kaleidoscope of colors, because their beauty and fragrance are beyond compare. One would think God had splashed paint and perfume all over the universe for us to enjoy. There are so many brilliant colors that no artist could ever capture such a spectacular sight.

To feel a warm breeze and see new life all around us is a blessing from God, but also very refreshing and invigorating. In my home state of West Virginia, there are many small towns among the beautiful rolling hills and winding valleys. Streams were crystal clear as they rippled along near the base of mountains. As water cascaded over rocks of various shapes and sizes, a babbling brook emerged as an invitation to children to come wading and cool off on a balmy day!

The Bennett family lived in one of those small towns in the southern part of the state just two miles south of Beckley. Homer Bennett and his wife, Gernie, shared a humble abode with their four children, a daughter, Dolores, who was the eldest, and three sons, Basil, Leroy and Homer, Jr.

This was the family I would be joining, and my mother was praying for a little girl with blonde hair and blue eyes. Weeks seemed to pass by very slowly as she waited for me to make my appearance. Day after day, she anxiously anticipated my arrival.

Then on April 3 as birds singing welcomed a new day and a mid-wife was on hand, the time came for me to meet my family. My mother was thrilled to have another daughter and her prayers were answered, because my eyes were blue-green and my hair would eventually be blonde. She named me Reba Nadine, but I was mostly called Nadine over the years. It was not long until my hair color was so light that my Uncle A.C. (Buck) called me "cotton top!"

Buck and his lovely wife, Nina, would visit occasionally and it was always a joy to have them stop by. Only a few years later, he followed in his brother's footsteps and joined the Navy, and to our family's dismay, their visits became few and far between. Buck was my dad's youngest brother, and there were others in between — Lundy, Clyde and Norman. They often came to visit and brought their families, too. My mother's brothers, Arless and Omar, and her sisters, Uversal and Ruby Jewel, also lived nearby. There were plenty of times our families got together and enjoyed homemade ice cream and other delicious goodies. Back then, almost everything was homemade and so delicious that it quickly disappeared!

My mother did not care much for pets, but when hungry stray dogs would come by, she would allow us to feed them. I recall a big black dog that came by one day and after being fed, he decided to stay. So, we named him Jock. Of course, he was not allowed in the house, but he was a very smart dog. He was even seen doing something that is hard to believe. There was a two-lane road that went through our small town of Crab Orchard, and when Jock wanted to cross to the other side, he actually looked both ways before he walked across! We considered him an intelligent dog!

When I was growing up, things were quite different from today with conveniences. Since no bus stopped at our front door, we walked the mile or so to grade school and did not mind it at all. Dolores called it shoe leather express! But, I often wondered over the years if we were influenced by our Cherokee heritage since my great, great grandmother was half Cherokee, and Native Americans were well known for swiftly traveling long distances by foot!

Winters were not severe in West Virginia, but occasionally a huge snowstorm blew through. We loved it when school was cancelled for the day and would pile the snow real high. Then we would hollow out the inside, and it became a snow-house. That was a real treat for us! We also enjoyed making snow angels just like children do today.

There was a hill in front of our house, and neighborhood children would gather to ride their sleds downhill. The boys would build a fire and burn old tires, which caused black smoke to fill the air and ascend toward the sky, but everyone could get warm before they trudged back up that hill just to ride back down again! It did not take much to entertain youth back in those days!

The Fourth of July was always an exciting holiday at our house, because Basil would buy skyrockets and sparklers, and there would be a wonderful display of fireworks in the front yard. Our neighbors also enjoyed the beautiful array of colors that filled the sky in celebration of our country's birth.

Since Crab Orchard was a small town, we knew most of the people that lived on the north side. One such family was the Byrd family. Their daughter, Mona, and I became friends and enjoyed spending time together. Her father, Robert Byrd, played a stringed instrument that country folks call the "fiddle." In cultured circles, it is referred to as a violin. News spread around that there would be a fiddling contest, and since my mother played the fiddle, she naturally entered the contest. She had been playing in public since ten years of age, and enjoyed it immensely, even though she could not read music. Mr. Byrd also entered the contest, and they tied for first place. That was a very exciting day in our lives! Later on, Mr. Byrd was elected Senator for the state of West Virginia. The family eventually moved away so he could pursue a career in politics.

Back in those days, one hardly ever heard someone say they were taking a vacation. If folks took trips, it was usually to visit relatives who lived in other cities or states. However, I do remember that on two separate occasions, we went to see the Atlantic Ocean. That was quite a treat for small children, but somewhat scary at the same time. Huge waves crashing toward us made us feel like they were going to swallow us up and carry us away. However, it was a tranquil experience to walk in the sand and camp near water. Hearing the rhythmic waves in the night is an awesome and peaceful sound.

Gernie Bennett was known as "The Fiddlin' Lady"
in West Virginia.

Chapter 2

Music In The Air

Members of our family were musically talented, especially my mother, who could play almost any stringed instrument she laid her hands on. My dad played the banjo. Together, they chose a few of their talented friends and started a band they called, "Homer Bennett and His Mocking Birds." They played their instruments and sang at various local social events.

Mankin Maddox played the mandolin and had a wonderful talent. George Abraham and his wife, Mary, also joined the band. Mary played the guitar and George the accordion. His talent was so fantastic that if he heard a song once, he could play it, much to everyone's amazement. Not one of them knew how to read music, but God had given each a gifted talent that enabled them to play "by ear." They were very popular and in demand all around the area.

We also have a distant cousin that was exceptionally musically inclined and could sing beautifully. Frances Octavia Smith was known in later years as an accomplished vocalist with the stage name of Dale Evans. She also wrote the song "Happy Trails" during her film career and marriage to Roy Rogers. That unforgettable song became the theme song to Rogers' television western program "The Roy Rogers Show," remembered today by many baby boomers.

Homer Bennett and his Mocking Birds

My parents also had a radio broadcast, and I always made it a point to be around when the group was practicing. At the radio station, I would lie on top of the old upright piano and watch with eager eyes. It was not long until it became apparent that I had music in my bones, too, and an unquenchable thirst for learning to play the piano. Since my family members played stringed instruments, there was no piano in our home. When my older brother Basil realized it, he scouted the area to find a used piano for me.

After he located one, the day finally came to pick it up. He and some friends took me with them to get it. I was so excited and anxious that I sat in the back of the pick-up truck on the piano bench and played "Chop Sticks" all the way home. Of course, that was the only song I knew how to play at the time. I did not know what the future would hold, but this was the beginning of my becoming an accomplished pianist that would lead to years of playing in church and eventually recording cassette tapes and CDs.

My daily routine became practicing the piano for one hour after supper every evening. But my sister, Dolores, ended up doing more than her share of dishes during those times. When asked what instrument she played, she always cheerfully responded over the years, "The radio!"

In the neighborhood, there was a farmer's young son of short stature named Jimmy who wanted to learn to play the guitar, so he asked Mr. John Cotton, who lived nearby, to teach him. Since he was so eager to learn, mastering the instrument was no chore at all. It was not long until he could play like the best. He wanted to become involved in the music industry, but didn't know how to go about it. When my dad heard the news, he invited Jimmy to play on one of his radio broadcasts. Jimmy was ecstatic and performed brilliantly. It wasn't long until "Little Jimmy Dickens" became household words, and it all came about by playing on a radio broadcast in Beckley, West Virginia with "Homer Bennett and His Mocking Birds."

Chapter 3

Living Off The Land

Our family grew almost all the food we ate. We planted a huge garden each summer, and there were berry bushes, grape vines and various fruit trees that produced delicious fruit. It was not easy work, but our labor provided many jars of jam and jelly, fruits and vegetables, which were stored on shelves in the cellar to last through long winter months.

We also had cows for beef and milk, hogs for pork, and chickens for poultry along with fresh eggs. Therefore, we did very little shopping in the local grocery store.

Mother made corn bread or biscuits every day with her meals and our family always enjoyed great food and good conversation around the kitchen table.

The family's favorite meal was a well-known southern dish called chicken and dumplings. When mother extended an invitation to someone to come to dinner for chicken and dumplings, that chicken was still walking around in the yard. Nothing compares to a meal made with fresh poultry.

As a child, I was really intrigued to observe hens tending to their fertilized eggs. They kept them warm for hours each day and before long hatched baby chicks.

To see new life peck through shells to freedom was like watching a miracle.

They were so tiny and quickly became covered with what looked like yellow fuzz; however, it took quite a while for their feathers to fully cover their bodies. They were so soft we couldn't help but cuddle them. Eggs were plentiful so my mother sold a few dozen each week to provide money for piano lessons for me.

Nadine at pre-school age.

After about one year of lessons, I could feel and hear other music inside me that wanted to come out through my fingers. My teacher wanted me to play only the notes in the music books, so I quit taking lessons and allowed God to develop the talent He had given me.

At almost any given time, if you walked past the Bennett house, you would hear me practicing by the hour. It was my favorite pastime, and my siblings often accused me of neglecting my chores. I also watched the technique of other pianists, and my talent began to develop quickly. It wasn't long until I was playing in church, much to my delight. Basil had a saxophone and could play beautifully. He allowed me to learn to play it, too, which I enjoyed immensely.

Chapter 4

The Revival Meeting That Changed Our Family

Most of our family attended a local church and seemed rather content, until one day when everything changed! Basil started working at the neighborhood grocery store owned and operated by Mr. Posey Rhodes. Basil was very reliable and anytime Mr. Rhodes needed someone for a special job, he would ask Basil to help him out. So Basil became his "right hand" man. This gentleman was a born-again Christian who attended a Full Gospel Church in Beckley, and he and his family lived just across the street from us. He was very congenial, and at one time or another, my sister, three brothers and I, all worked in his store.

There was a little playhouse in his back yard that his two daughters enjoyed. However, each morning before he became involved in the business of managing his store, he slipped out of his house and into the playhouse where he could be alone. There, he spent time in prayer because he felt his relationship with God was something that needed to be nurtured daily. He also knew that if he didn't take time before going to the store, the day would slip by and he would have no time for prayer. If a salesman or anyone else came to the office and asked to see Mr. Rhodes, his secretary told them he could not be disturbed at that time. They could wait to see him if they desired. They soon learned that if they wanted to talk to Mr. Rhodes, they should not expect him to be in his office first thing in the morning.

His desire was to see individuals come to know Christ as their Savior; however, Mr. Rhodes did not feel called to be a preacher. After much prayer and consideration as to what he could do personally to promote the Kingdom of God, he bought a school bus, and every time there was a church service, he drove that bus out through the hills and hollows of West Virginia, and allowed anyone that wanted to attend church to ride that bus free of charge.

When the church had a revival meeting, which meant that an evangelist would be called in to preach, there would be a church service every night except for Monday. That bus was seen going down the road and picking up people everywhere. There were times when the bus was full to over-flowing, which thrilled Mr. Rhodes. Just before arriving at the church, he would stop the bus and make a short speech. He would tell everyone that if they wanted to spend eternity in heaven, it was necessary to accept Jesus Christ as their personal Savior. No one will make it into heaven by just being good.

One night, there was an appointment he had to keep before the church service, so he asked Basil to drive the bus for him. Of course,

Basil was very happy to oblige. That night changed the lives of our family because Basil sat in that church service and heard the Plan of Salvation, which he had never heard in the nominal church he had attended for years. He came home and told mother that she should come to the church service the next night and hear this dynamic evangelist. He was so excited that she felt she needed to go see what made this young preacher so special.

During the next few nights, most of our family attended the church services and heard the Salvation Plan of how Jesus died on the cross to pay for our sins, and that all we had to do was repent of our sins and ask God to forgive us and accept Jesus as our personal Savior. It was so easy and simple to do, and my family members that were there accepted Christ as their Savior, including me. I was 12 years old at the time. From then on, we were faithful to attend church regularly, and also invited others to go along. My dad refused to go to church and we were heartbroken that he did not see his need for a Personal Savior, because without Salvation through Christ, there would be no eternity in heaven with his family!

The church usually had two revival meetings each year, and they were always well attended. Many individuals went to the altar to accept Christ as their Savior, and that was the thrilling part of it all. During one of those special meetings, a young evangelist and his wife came from the state of Kansas and brought with them their friend LaVaughn. She was a beautiful young lady with dark hair and brown eyes who sang solos, and was an exceptional pianist. She certainly was a wonderful addition to the services.

At that time, Basil was approximately 22 years old and a very handsome young man. Many young ladies in church had their eyes on him, but when he saw LaVaughn, he decided his search was over. Some months later they became engaged, and a wedding was being planned!

My dad was a hard worker and provided for the needs of his family. He was a mail carrier, and then purchased his own service station. By this time, he had built a lovely and spacious two-story brick home (below), which we enjoyed very much. After Basil and LaVaughn made their announcement to be married, Basil had a new house built for his bride. Leroy had joined the Air Force. So, our family was shrinking.

My sister, Dolores, had married her childhood sweetheart, but much to her dismay, he became very abusive. So after two years and two babies, a boy and a girl, she decided she should come home to live with the family again. Needless to say, she secured a job to earn a living, so guess who learned how to take care of babies? I really learned quickly, too, and loved it! Gary had hazel eyes and blonde hair, and Teresa had big brown eyes and dark hair, and it was not difficult to take care of them. We had a great time together.

You'll read a bit more about Teresa in this book, but let me first tell you a little more about her older brother. Gary loved to take things apart and could also figure out how to put them back together. When about four years old, he took apart the natural gas meter outside the house. Believing he would certainly be in trouble, he hid behind the sofa when the repairman came to put it back together.

Gary has an incredible ability to repair anything from tiny watches to vehicles and an inventive spirit to design items tailored to the need including a sophisticated alarm system. In keeping up with technology, he later became a computer expert.

Chapter 5

Moving To Pennsylvania

After accepting Christ as her Savior, my mother felt guilty when they played their instruments and sang for worldly entertainment. She felt she should use her talent for God, because He was the one that had given her this wonderful ability to play so many musical instruments. So, the group disbanded and went their separate ways. Dad did not want anything to do with this "religion" his family had found, and much to our dismay, he eventually left the family and moved to another town.

Then in 1953, mother decided to move to Pennsylvania where some of her family already resided. I had only two years of high school until I would graduate, and begged her to allow me to stay with my older brother, Basil and his wife LaVaughn, who lived nearby. However, my pleas fell on deaf ears and I was devastated to be leaving all my friends. There were three friends in particular I didn't want to leave. Carol Wray was a neighbor I had grown up with and when you saw one of us, you usually saw the other! We attended elementary school in Crab Orchard but there was no high school there, so we then had to ride the school bus to attend high school in Beckley. Rena Pittman was another friend that spent a lot of time at our home and she also attended the same church in Beckley.

When the Lively family moved to our community, their daughter, Norma Lee, asked a neighbor if there were any girls her age that lived nearby. The neighbor told her about our family. So, one day there was a knock on our door and Norma Lee and I liked each other right from the start.

Nadine, on left, is pictured with one of
her best friends, Norma Lee.

Surprisingly, we were the exact same age, even with the same birthday. We enjoyed teasing our friends and classmates by pretending to be twins. We were so much alike that we even amazed each other. On the day of our junior high school graduation, we discovered we had bought the exact same dress.

Carol, Rena and Norma were friends I did not want to leave. I would also be leaving my boyfriend behind, and I definitely was not happy about that! But, I had no choice in the matter, so it wasn't long until I was found packing my belongings.

Moving was somewhat of an adjustment for our family because we had always lived in West Virginia. We soon began to enjoy our new home, though, and made new friends in Mifflinburg, Pennsylvania. The town is located in the central part of the state in Union County, an area most associated with nearby Bucknell University.

Moving from West Virginia to north of the Mason-Dixon line in Pennsylvania was quite an experience, because we discovered that our newfound friends had quite an accent. Of course, those same friends thought we had an accent as well.

It was only a few weeks until I started attending high school in Mifflinburg, and right away the other students would laugh when I talked. I really didn't mind, because I found their accent quite amusing as well. However, it wasn't long until they would ask me to talk, just to hear my southern drawl. Southerners seem to keep part of their accent when moving to another state. In all my years, I have never lost all of mine!

Dolores was working when it came time for her children to start school, and since I was driving mother's Buick (mother always favored Buicks), I took them to school on their first day. However, I was unprepared for Teresa's stubbornness that day. Like most children, she did not want to stay so it took some coaxing. At that school, children started first grade because there was no kindergarten or preschool. Gary was cooperative since he was entering second grade and already familiar with school routine.

I would like to share an interesting story about my siblings and I calling our mother by the respectful name of mother since our childhood. She told us all as children that if we would call her mother instead of mom or mommy, she would give us a nickel. That was a lot of money back then, so, of course, we all eagerly agreed. She never did share her thoughts with us about why that was important to her.

Chapter 6

Finding A Church

One of our first objectives in our new surroundings was to find a church we could become a part of and join. So, we started attending and eventually became members of a small church in Milton.

Another noticeable difference between the north and south we quickly discovered is the way songs are sung in church. Down south they talk slowly but sing fast, and it is just the opposite in the north.

The first Sunday we were there, I went to the Teen Sunday School Class. Because I had always looked younger than my age, the teacher, a young man, took one look at me and asked, *"Don't you belong in the Junior Class?"* I looked up at him, and with a southern drawl replied, "Well, I'm sixteen," at which he responded, "Oh, then you *do* belong in this class."

I didn't know it yet, but I had just met my future husband and lifelong partner, and two years later Reba Nadine Bennett became Mrs. George Edward Van Riper, III.

It is rather ironic, though, that he first had eyes for my sister, Dolores, who also looked younger than her age. However, when he found out she was about five years older than he, and had been married with two children, he didn't feel he was quite ready for such a big responsibility.

When the church we attended held outdoor revival meetings in a tent out in the country, the pastor, interested in providing a variety of special soloists and vocalists each night, asked Teresa to sing a song at one of the services. She was only five-years-old at the time and I was 16. It also gave me the opportunity to accompany her on the piano, which I was happy to do. The family was very proud of her singing in front of a crowd at such a young age.

Chapter 7

George's Family

Almost three years before I made my appearance in this world, the Van Riper family was living in Sunbury, Pennsylvania. It was July 25, 1934, and they were celebrating the birth of their first son. They named him after his father, so he was called George Edward Van Riper, III. He already had a sister, Louise, and later on there would be five more children born into the family.

Growing up in a large family can be difficult at times, as it takes a great deal of money to provide for all the necessities in life. His family was by no means rich, but his mother did the best she could with what was available.

George can remember when she would buy a bag of jelly beans, and they had to be counted out into seven piles so each family member would get an equal number of pieces. He just knew he could eat the whole bag, but the confection had to be shared with the others.

When she bought a few cream puffs, she would have to cut them in half so everyone could have a piece. George loved them and could have eaten a half dozen, but he never had that luxury.

Mr. Van Riper secured a job in Milton, Pennsylvania and traveled there each Monday and stayed in town for the week. Aunt Mabel lived on Hepburn Street and had extra room so that provided room and board for him during his stay.

One week during the summer months, George was allowed to go with his father, and being about 12 years old, that was quite an adventure. His dad worked the 3 to 11 p.m. shift, so he was gone every evening.

One night George had nothing to do, so his dad gave him some money to attend the movies. Afterward, he went home but his Aunt Mabel was out for the evening. George really didn't want to be in that big house alone, so he pretended someone had broken in while he was gone. He ran down to the ACF (American Car Foundry) where his dad was a machinist. George ran inside and found his dad, and gasping for breath told him that someone had been in the house. His dad couldn't leave work right then, so he told George to wait until his shift ended and they would go home together.

Upon arriving at the house, they discovered someone actually had broken in, and that totally amazed George! His dad never did find out about that lie!

One hot summer day George and some friends wanted to go swimming, so they went down to the Susquehanna River and started wading in. George didn't know how to swim then, but he went along

44

with the rest. Pretty soon the water was above his waistline. The current became too strong to keep walking and carried him away. He could have drowned, but someone grabbed him and saved his life. He doesn't know who did it, but was surely grateful!

Chapter 8

Called Into The Ministry

George came from a rather large family, having one brother and five sisters. Louise was the oldest, after which George was born. Then along came Joyce, Bill, Barbara, Cheryl and Holly.

His mother, Mae, was a very sweet lady. She had many health problems and ended up having surgery approximately 15 times during her married life. Once, she fell backwards down the stairs and broke her back. She was in a cast for months. It was amazing that she survived that fall. As she grew older, she had to have a tracheotomy, at which time the doctor inserted a tube into her throat. In order to speak, she had to cover the tube with her hand and apply pressure. She lived with that for several years and it had to be difficult for her, but I never heard her complain.

They had lived in several different houses in Milton, but it was while they were living on Poplar Avenue, that a co-worker first invited Mr. Van Riper to go to church with him. At the time, they did not have a car and it was almost 15 miles from their house to the church. In those days, it took almost 30 minutes to drive that distance. However, Mr. Morehart volunteered to drive them to the service and back home again afterward. It was a Sunday morning and the whole family attended the service that day, except for George and Bill, who were visiting with Grandpa and Grandma Van Riper for the weekend.

George and Mae Van Riper listened carefully to the songs and sermon, and realized something was missing in their lives. They felt convicted and knew they should repent of their sins. So, they walked down the aisle to the altar and the pastor led them in the sinner's prayer and they accepted Christ as their Lord and Savior.

Afterward, they knew in their hearts they had been changed, and wanted this same change for their boys. So, they called Grandma Van Riper and told her the boys must come home that afternoon so they could attend the service that evening. Of course, George and Bill didn't want to return home, because they considered themselves to be on vacation. They were surprised to hear their parents had gone to church that morning, and were even more amazed they were going back that evening and wanted their sons to go with them. They had no desire to go to church, however, they also knew that when their dad spoke, they had better listen or they were in big trouble. So, Grandpa Van Riper drove them home that afternoon.

That evening Mr. Morehart came for them, and all seven piled into his car. Some of the younger ones had no place to sit, except on someone's lap. (Seatbelts had not yet been installed in vehicles.)

But, they seemed to manage and off they went to church. The pastor was very happy to see them and welcomed them to the service. That night, there was a quartet there from Eastern Bible Institute and they sang several songs. Then, one of them spoke and preached a "Salvation Message," and related a story of a young man who would not accept Christ, and death came early in his life. He was not taken by the angels into heaven, but by Satan into hell where he suffered flames and torment. By this time, George was sitting on the edge of his seat and totally enraptured by what he heard.

He realized the story was true and he did not want to spend eternity in hell. As a 14-year-old lad, he was scared and trembling, and quickly walked down the aisle to the altar when the invitation was given. The pastor prayed with him and he repented of his sins and asked Jesus to come into his heart. He knew his life was changed and that "old things had passed away, and everything became new."

It was hard for him to explain just how he felt as he left church that night, but he felt light as a feather and as though a heavy weight had been lifted from him. It brought back to mind how he would wake up many times in the middle of the night and walk into the bathroom. He would look into the mirror and say, "George, if you died tonight, where would you spend eternity?" It always made him feel scared and he didn't know what to do about it, but now he knew that if he died, he would go to heaven to be with Jesus. That certainly was a wonderful feeling! That night he woke up, but was not afraid, and was actually praising God and saying "hallelujah!"

He was eager to tell his friends he was a born-again Christian; however, some of them just laughed and made fun of him because they didn't understand what he was talking about. Their taunting caused him to stop talking about his new found "Friend" for a while, and that was a big mistake, which made him feel ashamed. Later on, he began to witness for Jesus again, and told his friends how God had changed his life the night he knelt at an altar of prayer and accepted Christ as His Lord and Savior. He wanted his friends to accept Jesus, too.

This "new birth" changed him in many ways, and his friends saw a difference in him. Before, he was guilty of stealing and lying. All of a sudden, he didn't want to do those things anymore, because he knew it would displease God. He knew he shouldn't steal cigarettes from his Grandpa anymore. Before this time, when he did steal some, he and Bill took them down by the pond and climbed up into a tree to smoke. The first time he inhaled, George couldn't get his breath and almost fell out of the tree.

Another time, he was down by the creek and tried once again to smoke a cigarette, and the same thing happened—he couldn't breathe. He was splashing water into his mouth, and trying everything he could think of in order to catch his breath. He began to wonder why anyone would want to smoke anyway, as it certainly was not a pleasant experience. Furthermore, it is very detrimental to good health.

The Van Riper family started attending all the services at church, and different church members would take turns coming to pick them up. There were four services each week, and they didn't want to miss any of them. Of course, there were times the children didn't want to stop playing on Sunday afternoon to get ready to go. However, they went anyway because dad said so.

During those years at home in Milton, George enjoyed the outdoors and loved animals. Here is his description of the menagerie he tended in the family's backyard.

There was a shed at the back of our yard where we lived on Poplar Avenue that I claimed for my domain. I had chickens, hamsters, pigeons, white mice, bantam hens, rabbits, a cat and a dog. It sounds like it would be a crowded shed, but actually there was space for a lounge chair and potbellied stove. It was a very cozy hideaway. I spent many hours there with my good friend Tony Botto, my older sister's father-in-law.

I had a nice vegetable garden in our backyard and raised different vegetables my family enjoyed during the summer. I really thought I wanted to be a farmer, but God had other plans for my life.

After accepting Christ, George took time to read the Bible and pray each day because he wanted his life to be pleasing in God's sight. Then one day as he was painting the front porch of his Aunt Mabel's house, he knew in his heart that God wanted him to be a minister. He knew he had much to learn if he was going to be the vessel God wanted him to be. From that day forward, he began to

make plans to attend Bible school. Here is his account of the day
God called him into the ministry.

I remember it quite well. One afternoon when I was painting my
Aunt Mabel's front porch banister, I was thinking of what I wanted
to be and The Holy Spirit spoke to my heart and said, "Go You into
all the world and preach."

I didn't hear an audible voice, but I knew God had laid His hand
on me for the ministry. It was rather surprising because I was very
shy as far as any public speaking was concerned. I was not the most
qualified candidate for the ministry. But, God does not call the qualified; He qualifies those He calls. I had no idea what the ministry was
or how to preach or what might be involved, but I did know God
said, "*Go You into all the world and preach.*"

At the time, I didn't know this calling would take my wife,
Nadine, who would come into my life later, halfway around the
world to India on a preaching mission, and into over 22 states as
evangelists, and pastorates in five states. When we were traveling as
evangelists, we put over 50,000 miles on our car in two consecutive
years. We are eternally grateful that in all those miles, we never had
a serious accident.

George was about 15 years old then, but from that moment
he knew his life's calling was to be a minister of the gospel. He
planned to study to be approved unto God, a workman that need not

be ashamed. He was still in high school and would wait three years before being able to attend Bible college.

He received a unique opportunity before even attending Bible school. Various churches in the Milton area invited George to preach to their small congregations to gain early experience. His shyness seemed to fade away.

Chapter 9

Grandma Amey

Quite often, the family would go to visit Mae's mother, Grandma Carrie Amey, who was one of the sweetest individuals you would ever want to meet. She lived in Shamokin, Pennsylvania, which is at the western edge of the anthracite coal-mining region in Northumberland County. The small town was incorporated as a borough in 1864 and as a city in 1949. This industrious town was also known for its silk and knitting mills, stocking and shirt factories, wagon shops, ironworks, and brickyards.

Grandma Amey took care of her aged mother, Great Grandma Michael, who was also a sweetheart. Sometimes when folks get older they have a tendency to get cranky, but not these two ladies. It was always a pleasure to visit with them, and there were always some homemade goodies in the kitchen for everyone to enjoy. George was always elated when Grandma Amey made molasses cookies, because that was one of his favorites.

When George was just a little tyke, he would go up to the third floor with Grandma Michael because he loved to hear her pray aloud, which was always in Dutch. If she would forget and pray silently, he would beg her to pray out loud so he could again hear her pray in Dutch. He actually learned to speak some of the words, but over the years has forgotten most of them.

Beyond Grandma's backyard was a little lane and beyond that a small stream, which always looked black because there was a huge mountain of coal dust right behind it. The coal dust actually looked like black sand. Almost every day miners would dig coal, and the mountain would grow taller and taller. Naturally, some of it would fall down into the stream, which gave it the shocking appearance of black ink. George and Bill loved to go back there and throw sticks or anything else they could find into the water.

One Sunday afternoon the family was visiting with Grandma, and the boys went out to play. Their dad told them to stay away from the water and they tried to do so, but it just looked too tempting. So, they slowly made their way to the bank of the stream, and began to throw sticks and empty cans into the water, which was about ten feet below. Once in a while they would look back toward the house to see if their dad had come outside, but so far, so good.

They found a small log and decided it might float, which would be fun to watch, so they tossed it into the water. It got caught on something and they wanted it to float so badly that they scrambled down the bank to push the log out into the middle of the stream.

When they reached the edge of the water, they could see it was all murky and sticky, and there was mud everywhere.

When Bill stepped into it, his foot and leg disappeared all the way up to his hip. When he pulled his leg out, he was minus a shoe. They knew they were in trouble, so George reached down into the hole to get Bill's shoe, and that is when he looked back up the hill and saw his dad watching them. Naturally, his arm was all black and dirty, and he hadn't found the shoe! They knew then that punishment was inevitable.

Their dad allowed them to choose their own punishment. They could take a spanking or be grounded for two weeks. Bill did not want to be grounded, so he chose to be spanked. He figured that it would be over in a few minutes, and then he would be free to do what he wanted. On the other hand, George did not want a spanking because he did not like pain, so he chose to stay in the yard for two weeks. Those were probably the longest two weeks of his life!

Chapter 10

The Van Riper Family

When we first started dating, the Van Riper family lived about ten miles outside of Milton in a one-room schoolhouse. The back part of the house had been petitioned off into four bedrooms, but the walls did not reach the ceiling. There was a hallway and the rest of the area housed the living room and kitchen. There was heat but it did not reach back to the bedrooms. One night the boys wanted to see just how cold it was in their room, so they put a pan of water on the floor by the bed. When they awoke the next morning, the water had completely frozen! Now, that was a cold bedroom!

There was no running water in the house, so George and Bill took turns carrying water from the well at the landlord's house, which was about 1,000 yards away. One evening they needed water and it was Bill's turn to get it. It was already dark outside and Bill didn't really want to go, but he picked up two buckets and hurried to the well. Once he had filled them, he had to walk slowly back to the house so the water would not splash out.

Meanwhile, his brother, George, thought he would play a trick on Bill and picked up his 16-gauge shotgun and loaded it. He waited outside near their house, and when Bill was about 20 feet away, George shot the gun into the air, and yelled, "Get him, boys!" Well, it scared Bill so badly that he dropped both buckets and the grass in that area was well watered! He ran to the house just as fast as his legs would carry him, and tried to tell his parents what had happened. As he stood there gasping for breath, George came through the door laughing so hard he almost dropped his gun. However, his laughing stopped abruptly when he heard his Dad's stern words, *"Now, son, you go get the water."*

While George was still in high school, he took a job at the Buffalo Valley Dairy on Hepburn Street in Milton delivering milk. Back then, milk was delivered door to door at homes and the glass bottles were placed next to the door in small metal insulated containers.

Every other day he was out of bed by 3 a.m. and went to the dairy, picked up his moneybag, loaded the truck with milk, and started his route by 4 a.m. Since his job began so early, he had access to the key, so he opened the plant every morning. After school, he returned to the dairy to dip ice cream for customers from 4 to 6 p.m. He actually ate so much while employed there, that he couldn't eat ice cream for years.

George, left, is pictured with his brother Bill
in the backyard of their Grandma Amey's home.

One morning when he opened the plant, he looked inside and noticed the cabinet door was open where the moneybags were kept. He knew someone had broken into the plant and quickly called his boss, but the boss was unavailable so he spoke with his son. The son told George to go ahead and load the truck and make his deliveries, and that he would call the police. When the police arrived, they found the perpetrator still hiding in the building. It turned out to be a former employee who was a very large man that had an emotional problem resulting from an accident and head injury. We were grateful for God's protection that day.

Another morning, George's brother Bill went with him on his route, and everything was going well until the left rear wheel came off the truck. When that wheel fell off, George lost control of the truck. It veered off the road to the right and climbed a small knoll, which caused bottles of milk to spill out of the truck. Since they were made of glass, it caused quite a mess! Bill was scared half to death and decided not to help anymore.

During his high school years, George was very athletic and played Junior Varsity Basketball. He was good enough to be on the "first string" for a while, which he enjoyed very much. He was a very good player and became a hero in the eyes of some of the teenage girls, which really fed his ego!

George attended high school through the eleventh grade, and then in 1952, he went for three days to his senior class. His family was rather poor and he wanted to help earn some money, so he quit school and got a job with the Pennsylvania Railroad Company. His position was called a gandy dancer back then, and with a crew of men, they raised track, tamped ballast, drove spikes and replaced ties and rails. When they worked during winter months, there were times when temperatures were so bitterly cold, it caused the jack-hammers to freeze up. The men would then have to thaw them out by using a blowtorch. George only weighed about 150 pounds then, and when he was using a jackhammer, you couldn't tell which was shaking the most, him or the hammer!

One day while working with the track gang out of Montgomery, Pennsylvania, the crew had been raising track and had several jacks in place under the rail. When the watchman signaled to the men that a freight train was coming, they quickly loosened the jacks, took their jackhammers and moved aside to let the train pass.

They were all shocked when one of the men shouted, "We missed one jack!" One of them ran to release the jack and threw it aside just as the train soared past. That could have been a terrible tragedy that day if he hadn't noticed the jack in time and the train hit it. Had that happened, the train could have derailed and caused severe injuries. Thank God for sending an angel to protect George and the others. The gandy dancer teams have since been replaced by a single machine that pulls and drives spikes, tamps the ballast, raises and shifts tracks automatically.

During winter that year, the Montgomery Plant closed down, and the men were transferred to South Williamsport. The night before George was to report to work, he had stayed up very late and grew very sleepy as he drove to work that morning. As he neared South Williamsport, he was traveling down Penny Hill when he fell asleep at the wheel. The next thing he heard was the car hitting the guide rail, which wrapped around his bumper and kept him from going down a steep hillside and crashing at the bottom. Once again, God had sent His angel to spare George's life. Here is the scripture that immediately came to George's mind early that morning.

Psalms 34:7 The angel of the Lord encampeth round about those who fear him, and delivereth them.

George couldn't stay with that job since he no longer had transportation, and since he enjoyed working with wood, got a job at the Milton Cabinet Company where he made television cabinets. His work required him to use an overhead router and a 15-inch direct drive table saw. He later left that job when it was time to attend Bible school.

Since they lived out in the country and only had one car, he had to move into Milton in order to have transportation to work. His pastor, Paul Pittman, invited him to stay with his family because they lived near the factory and George could walk to work from there. He enjoyed working with wood, so he excelled at his job.

Many times his boss would ask him to work overtime in order to get extra work done that day. He would always try to oblige, unless there was a church service that night. It upset his boss that George would prefer going to church rather than earning extra money; however, this young man felt it was very important to attend Bible Study on Wednesday evenings.

George learned that Pastor Pittman needed to supplement his income, so George put in a good word for him at the factory and they promptly hired him. One day shortly after lunchtime, he was working very diligently when Pastor Pittman received a telephone call from his wife who sounded quite upset and with good reason. Their young son, David, had swallowed a penny and it was lodged in his throat. The pastor left immediately to rush his child to the emergency room at the hospital. A short time later, George felt led to stop working and pray for this child. He looked at his watch after praying and remembered the exact moment, which was 1:22 p.m.

Later that afternoon, Pastor Pittman came back to work and was asked how David was doing. He told them the penny would not budge and it was becoming a very serious situation, until exactly at 1:22 p.m. when the child swallowed the coin. God had heard and answered prayer! It is so important to be obedient when God speaks to our hearts, to stop what we are doing and pray. We should never minimize the power of prayer.

Chapter 11

My First Real Beau

When I first met my husband-to-be, he really didn't appeal to me, but when he asked me for a date, I did agree to go out with him.

George and Nadine at the Van Riper country home in Milton.

It's a wonder that I ever dated him again, because he was about two hours late for our first date! I thought he was not going to show up, but later found out the men of the church were building a new structure and worked late that evening, and he was helping them. How could I be upset with that? It told me a great deal about his character.

When he finally came, my mother had loads of questions for him to answer, so it was getting late when we finally went out. It was a short date, because I had to be in by eleven o'clock; however, everything went well and we enjoyed the brief time we had together. There were other dates and as time passed, we learned to know each other better and began to fall in love.

One day he brought a gift to me, and when I opened the package, I saw a beautiful wrist watch. I was proud to wear it knowing he had picked it out just for me!

My brother, Junior, was unable to wear a watch because as soon as he put one on his wrist, it would begin to run erratically. None of us knew exactly why that happened, but it didn't disturb him and he just never wore one. I will forever remember one Sunday afternoon when he asked to borrow my new watch because he and a friend wanted to take a ride into the mountains, and they wanted to be sure to get back in time to attend the church service that evening. I told him he could borrow it, but he had to be really careful with it. He agreed and put it in his shirt pocket. Then they hopped into his pick-up truck and headed for the mountains.

They not only enjoyed driving up narrow mountain roads looking for wildlife, but also walking through the woods to catch sight of animals in their natural habitat. They tried to walk quietly as they scanned the surrounding area, but occasionally they could hear the leaves crackling under their feet. Then all of a sudden, they saw a bear, and at the same moment, it saw them. They turned to run, and the bear began to chase them! What a scary moment they had! They ran as fast as they could, but Junior slipped and fell. He jumped up, turned and looked back, and sure enough the bear was gaining on him. They raced to the truck, jumped inside and slammed the door shut just in time! What a relief it was to be out of reach of danger! At that point, they were ready to head for home!

When they walked into the house, they had a story to tell! They were still very excited about their adventure, and we were glad they were home and safe. After they quieted down a little bit, I looked at Junior and asked, "Where is my watch?" He reached into his pocket and said, "Oh, no! It must have fallen out when I fell down in the forest."

He knew what he had to do, so he looked at his friend and said, *"Let's go!"* They drove back up the mountainside and parked the truck. I am sure that *some* prayers were going up to our Heavenly Father for help in this situation. What would he do if he couldn't find it? He didn't know, so they frantically looked for the place where he had fallen, and they were sure they had found it. But, where was the watch? As they looked all around, it didn't take long for their eyes to fall upon the right spot. There was the watch, neatly wrapped around a leaf, just as though it was waiting for them. Junior was so relieved as he picked it up and hurried home. When they arrived and walked in the door, his face told me what I wanted to know, and I was so grateful! God is so good!

George and my youngest brother, Junior, became very good friends. One day, they decided to imitate Tom Sawyer and Huckleberry Finn. So, they built a raft. Not knowing what materials to use, they chose creosote railroad ties, and tongue and groove yellow pine flooring. Of course, the raft ended up being very heavy, and when they pushed it into the Susquehanna River, it sank. They pulled it out and attached some square five-gallon cans on the bottom trusting it to float.

They pushed it back into the river and climbed aboard. They were so excited! They were having a great time and it actually stayed afloat. But, when they hit the rapids, the cans scraped on rocks. As the cans began to fill with water, the raft began to sink. There was a bridge up ahead and people were lined up watching this great river adventure. They were even cheering them on. To the boys' dismay, their raft sank to the bottom of the river. The water was not very deep in that area, so they simply walked to shore. They were so disappointed their adventure ended so abruptly, but still enjoyed the time they were floating downriver.

Chapter 12

Starting Bible School

It wasn't long after we started dating that George and I began to sing duets together. We were invited to some neighboring churches and after singing together, he preached. My years of practicing the piano were rewarded and God blessed in these services. Little did we know, this was the beginning of our singing career, all according to His plan.

When fall arrived, it was time for George to pack his bags and head for Bible school in Rhode Island. We had only known each other for six weeks, and it must have been God's Will for us to be together because we were actually just getting acquainted.

On his last Sunday at his home church in Milton, the pastor encouraged the congregation to give him a "Pentecostal Handshake" to help him on his way. In case you have never heard that term, it means you should have some money in your hand, which you would leave in his hand after the handshake. Therefore, when he arrived at school, he had some cash in his pockets. However, since it was a faith school and everyone trusted God every day for their food and other needs, he gave all of his money in the offerings.

When he first arrived at Zion Bible Institute in East Providence, there was no one there he knew, so he immediately began to get acquainted with some of the other students. Since he wasn't the only new student there, and being a very out-going type person, he had no trouble making new friends.

He was late getting to the first meal, which was dinner, and felt rather embarrassed that he had to sit at the faculty table because that was the only empty seat in the dining room. He felt even worse when he saw the main course was macaroni and cheese, which he usually wouldn't eat. (He did not and still does not like cheese!) He was a healthy young man who was very hungry, and not wanting to seem ungrateful for the food, he proceeded to take a bite of the entrée and then stuff a huge piece of bread in his mouth, hoping that it would help to kill the taste of the cheese! I don't think it helped very much, and I know he was thrilled when that meal was over and he could leave the table.

He came home only two or three times a year from Rhode Island, which was about an eight-hour drive, and he did not have a car. If he wanted to come home for a visit, he had to hitchhike because he had no money for bus fare.

One time when he came home for a visit, he brought his friend, Lou Jensen, with him. It took most of the night for them to get a ride, so they had very little sleep. In fact, they were so cold and tired at one point, that no matter which way a car was traveling, they tried to hitch a ride just so they could finally get in out of the cold. A man stopped and picked them up, but it was only a matter of minutes until they realized that it was a mistake to accept that ride, because the man was drunk and the car started to weave all over the road to the point that it became very dangerous. Needless to say, they did a lot of praying, and got out of that car as quickly as they possibly could!

When they arrived at my home, George borrowed my mother's car so he could pick me up at high school. Because of the lack of sleep, his eyes were blood-shot, and to say that he looked good would have stretched the truth drastically! But, he wanted to see me, so I had to give him credit for making the effort to come home, no matter how he looked!

He came to our house one day and asked me to go for a ride with him into the country. Once he reached a serene setting, he stopped the car, opened the door and asked me to step out for a minute. Then he knelt before me and to my surprise, he proposed! I accepted and he put a beautiful engagement ring on my finger! Then we drove back to my house to announce our engagement! What an exciting day that turned out to be!

George studied very hard and excelled in his classes during the two years he attended Zion Bible Institute in East Providence, Rhode Island. Meanwhile, I finished my last two years of high school. My graduation ceremony was scheduled for Thursday evening, May 26, 1955, and our wedding was planned for the following Sunday after-noon. We had originally planned a June wedding, but when we were invited to hold a revival meeting in El Dorado, Kansas the second week of June, we changed our wedding date to May 29, 1955. That way there would be plenty of time for a honeymoon before the trip to the mid-west.

My future husband had few opportunities to come home while attending Bible school; however, when my Grandpa Huffman passed away, he was able to attend the funeral. Also, mother's brothers, Arless and Omar, and her sisters, Ruby Jewell, and Uversal (everyone called her Verse) were all there with their children. It was a sad time, but Grandpa had lived a long and full life, so that gave us some comfort.

It is a wonder that my newfound beau ever called on me again after meeting some of my relatives. Not that there was anything wrong with them, because they were wonderful people, but some accidents in life had left their mark. My Uncle Arless had stepped into a mill grinder when he was younger, and his left leg from the knee down was destroyed. The doctors had a prosthesis made for him and he tried to wear it, but it was so heavy that it wore him out just walking around. So, he decided to make a new one for himself.

Actually, he took some wood and made a peg leg. When he sat down, the leg stuck straight out, but he didn't mind until one day when he had to catch a bus to town. He sat down on the front seat, but there was no room in front of him to put his leg. If he sat with it in the aisle, it was in the way of other passengers. So, he decided to make another one and put a small hinge on the back of it in the area of the knee, and all he had to do when he sat down was hit the wooden leg in the back and it dropped down to the floor. It was rather comical at first, but Uncle Arless just laughed along with the rest of us, and pretty soon we did not give it a second thought.

My Uncle Omar could play the rhythm guitar very well until he had an accident with a gun and lost half of his left hand. After it healed, he still had his thumb and fore finger, so he learned to play the Hawaiian guitar. He loved music, and wasn't going to let anything deter him from doing something he dearly loved.

Both of these uncles had lamb chop sideburns and loved cowboy hats, so when they came to town for Grandpa's Huffman's funeral, they proudly displayed them. After the funeral service was over, everyone went back to our house. Since music had been such a vital part of our lives and we had all grown up on country music, I sat down at the piano, my mother picked up her fiddle, her brothers grabbed guitars, and Verse's husband, Grover, sat down with a banjo on his knee, and we all started playing a song called, *"Sugar Foot Rag."* Everyone was tapping their feet to the music, except for Uncle Grover, who never moved a muscle and never cracked a smile the whole time we played music. However, he surely loved to play that banjo and did a great job. There was a lot of talent in that room, and the music really sounded professional. I cannot remember my grandparents ever playing any musical instruments, but their children surely were blessed with wonderful talents!

Mother's grandchildren also gathered around to hear these music sessions. The song they most requested was to play the lively and energized "Orange Blossom Special" because they especially loved to hear my mother mimic the sound of a train whistle on her fiddle. With the guitars and banjo along with the fiddle, the combined talent was truly awesome and equal to any country music band performance at the Grand Ole Opry in Nashville. Done bluegrass style as an instrumental, it seemed to be the children's favorite. However, there *are* lyrics to this song about a passenger train.

Well, my future husband did not quite know what to think about all of this, because when he accepted Christ as His Lord and Savior, he gave up all music except for gospel music. He had a very delicate stomach and actually got sick, and had to go lie down when he heard us playing country music. Sometimes, God deals with hearts in different ways and there are times when it is better to eliminate some things from our lives rather than continue doing them, and possibly become a stumbling block to someone else. Eventually, the only music I played was southern gospel and church hymns that are, in my opinion, the best music around!

Chapter 13

Our Wedding Day

After school and on Saturdays, I worked part time at a grocery store and tried to save a little bit of money. Back then, wages were very minimal and since there was very little cash available, we had to make do the best we could in planning for the wedding. A lack of finances did not stop us from having a wonderful and lovely wedding. Basil and LaVaughn bought a new suit for George, and our pastor's wife, Mrs. Arlene Garman, loaned me her beautiful wedding gown. LaVaughn allowed me use of her bridal veil, so in borrowed clothing, I became a bride that Sunday afternoon!

My mother and Dolores also helped me tremendously with the work involved in planning for a wedding shower as well as a ceremony. Much to my amazement, one of my school teachers came, and there was also five of our minister friends there, which was delightful.

The wedding took place in Mifflinburg where we lived. The pastor of our church, Rev. Howard Garman officiated and in the absence of my dad, my brother Basil walked down the aisle with me, and "*gave me away.*" The wedding took place at 3 p.m. and everything was going very well, until during the ceremony when a severe storm moved in very quickly and lightning filled the sky. While thunder rumbled outside, it did not interfere with the ceremony, but did present problems afterward.

My brother, Junior, had borrowed an antique car from a friend and if memory serves me was a 1932 Buick. It was a convertible that was a confederate model, meaning the spare tire was on the rear bumper instead of on the side on the running board behind the front fender.

Nadine's brother Basil is cranking the engine to get the antique car started so the wedding couple can make the customary drive through town on their way to the reception.

We planned to ride in the rumble seat and drive through town. However, the storm made that impossible, so we rode in the back seat instead with the top up, dragging behind us several empty Texaco Motor Oil cans to create some celebratory racket.

The traditional "Just Married" sign was reattached to the trunk lid after the rainstorm and was mostly visible behind the spare tire. Below the tire in the center of the bumper was the owner's amusing sticker that read: *Don't honk!* I know the light is green.

Then, when we tried to drive to the place where the reception was to be held, we found out the street was blocked by a tree that had been struck by lightning, so we had to find another way to get there. We had also planned an outdoor reception, which had to be moved indoors. What a way to start a life together!

Bennett and Van Riper family members give
the wedding couple a happy sendoff.

We could not afford to buy a car, so our brother-in-law, James Botto, helped us to finance our first automobile. We were so grateful for his kindness. God has been so good and has blessed us in so many ways! We have found that God always meets the needs of His children when they trust Him, no matter how large or how small the need may be.

From left are, front row: George's Grandma Amey and Great Grandma Michael, Nadine and George, and Nadine's Grandma Huffman. Second row, from left: George's paternal Grandma Van Riper, George Van Riper, II, George's mother Mae, and Nadine's mother Gernie Bennett.

Our honeymoon consisted of a few days at Watkins Glen in New York, a scenic area with waterfalls, a gorge and much rich history. On the second day, my husband discovered big red blotches on his body, and we later found out it was hives. That put a slight damper on our honeymoon, and made life rather interesting for a few days. He was terribly embarrassed, but neither of us knew anything about hives at that time, so we had no clue as to what was wrong with him.

After our honeymoon, we again packed our suitcases and headed for El Dorado, Kansas for our first *revival meeting*. We didn't know anyone there, but the pastor was the father of my sister-in-law, LaVaughn. He and his wife were so cordial and encouraged us by inviting us to come to their church to minister to their congregation. The trip took many hours, because back then, there were no inter-state highways, and roads went through every little town on the way. In fact, some of the towns still had wooden sidewalks, and that was a delightful surprise. My brother Leroy had also gone to Bible school and he went with us on this trip. His car was newer than ours, so we took it, which was a blessing and the trip went very well.

We had never traveled across the United States, so we were in for a treat. As we drove through Ohio, we noticed there were still some hills and valleys, but the mountains seemed to have disappeared. By the time we arrived in Indiana, the hills and valleys were gone, too. The ground was so flat, we could see for miles. It certainly was different from the northeast. Isn't it amazing that God would create such a beautiful and unusual world just for us to live in and enjoy?!

By this time, we had bought an accordion, which I played when we sang duets, and my husband played the rhythm guitar. With being married such a short time, some folks in the congregation commented they could see the love we had for each other in our eyes, as George picked up my accordion and handed it to me, and we sang together. However, sometimes it was rather comical when we sang, because the longer the song, the faster he played. There were times when I could hardly keep up with him. Eventually, I laid down the accordion and started playing the piano for our accompaniment.

The revival meetings went very well, and God gave us a good harvest of souls. After all, that's what it is all about anyway! After the meetings were over, we made our way back to Pennsylvania, and then began to make plans for George to finish his Bible school training. That was something he felt was very important to do before entering into full time ministry.

Chapter 14

Bible School Days

My mother was a great cook. After dating me and eating her cooking, I am sure my husband was amazed to find out I could not cook a lick! Mother did not want anyone underfoot when she was working in the kitchen, so all I learned how to do was set the table and fill the water glasses. Of course, I helped clean up after the meal and I did my share of cleaning the house each week.

It was only a few months after our wedding that we left Mifflinburg and traveled to Green Lane, Pennsylvania. George wanted to finish his last year of Bible school training there because they had room for married students. He had already attended Zion Bible Institute in East Providence, Rhode Island for two years. It was a Faith School, and students had to learn to trust God for their daily needs, which would certainly be an asset for our future in the ministry. He had worked in the kitchen at that school and learned a lot about cooking. Therefore, he was able to help me as I learned to cook. Those first meals I prepared were something to remember, or I should say, forget!

We moved into a small cottage on school grounds and had been able to purchase a mohair couch and chair for $12. Somehow we managed to secure a table and two chairs. My mother had given us my bedroom suite to take with us, which was wonderful! We could not afford a refrigerator, so we had an icebox.

Depending on your age, you may not even know what that is or how it works! It was made somewhat like a refrigerator with two doors on the front and insulated. The top section held a huge chunk of ice, which cooled the food in the bottom section. The ice melted away, and then you had to replace it in order to keep food cold. We knew very little about it at the time, and one day we became very ill after eating some meat that had not been kept cold enough. However, this time of "living by faith" would prepare us for the ministry in future years, because we would be confronted many times when "faith in God" would be our only answer.

It was not long until we discovered we were expecting our first baby. We did not have money to buy maternity clothes, so my mother was kind enough to make some for me. She was an excellent seamstress and the dresses were beautiful. In fact, as I was growing up, she made just about all my clothes. The first store-bought dress I can remember was for my junior high school graduation.

Several of the men that attended Bible school, including my husband, took part time jobs at a furniture factory, which helped with our expenses and put food on the table. He brought home the huge sum of $25 each week and believe me, that was not a big salary even though it was back in 1956.

Chapter 15

Our First Child

Old Man Winter made his appearance once again, and we had our share of snow and cold temperatures. One day, it began to snow and seemed it would never stop. When the last flake made its way to the ground, a total of 28 inches had fallen and everything was clothed in pure white. No one would be driving anywhere for a day or two. It took quite a while for that huge blanket of snow to melt away, and for the ground to be seen once again.

Soon temperatures began to rise, and cold air was only a memory. As warm breezes began to blow again, winter faded into the background and the smell of spring filled the air. Soon the sweet odor of apple blossoms would permeate the air, and beautiful flowers would add their fragrance! It was so refreshing to experience after being cooped up in the house for so long.

There was one humorous incident that happened while we were there. We were coming back from town one day and George decided to stop at the Bible School's Administration Building for a few moments. Being "great with child," I waited in the car. (This term comes from the Bible when Mary was pregnant with Jesus.) Because of his habit of going to our cottage from his classes each day, he forgot about me and left the building by the back door.

As he neared our home, he noticed the car was gone, and immediately thought, "Oh, my goodness, Nadine has driven herself to the hospital!" He ran frantically through the cottage, calling my name. When he could not find me anywhere, he then ran around the circle of houses to the homes of our friends to ask if they had seen me. Of course, no one had! Finally, he reached a spot in the road where he could see our car, and he could not believe what he had just done! He felt like he was about an inch tall. Needless to say, our friends did not let him forget that incident for weeks to come!

Time seemed to drag along as we anxiously awaited the arrival of our first child. Then one day, I told George he should call the doctor because my labor pains had started. Being our first child, we did not know just how quickly the baby would come, so we went to the hospital many hours before we should have gone. The time seemed endless to my husband as he paced the floor waiting for some news. They told him the baby would not be born for several hours and he should go home. But, he did not want to leave the hospital until the baby was born. He thought that night would never end.

The delivery was difficult and I was awake the whole time because the doctor—if you can call him that—gave me *nothing* for pain. After labor pains had started, it was 25 hours before our son made his appearance, only 11 months after our wedding

It was in the early morning hours of April 17, 1956 when a cry was heard in the delivery room as a new life came into the world. Nevin George was born weighing nine pounds and eleven ounces. He had very little hair and George favored the name Josephus, and we even considered George Van Riper, IV, but later decided on what was an unusual name at the time, Nevin, and gave him George for his middle name. Surprisingly, Nevin has remarked over the years that he would have loved being named after his father.

Nevin was very healthy and perfect in every way, but we found out very quickly that he was allergic to the formulas recommended by the doctor. Life became very trying and interesting for several months as we tried formula after formula, but he could not keep any of them down. Finally, in desperation we gave him whole milk, and thank God, after a while he adjusted to it.

Looking back on that painful delivery and long hours in labor, I recall we were not sure if we ever wanted to have another child. Of course, like every couple, that feeling changed as soon as we cuddled our beautiful newborn in our arms and looked into that adorable little face. We also thanked God the doctor's fee was very minimal and we were able to cover the cost.

My mother came to our little cottage and stayed for about a week to help me. After having five children of her own, there was no doubt in my mind she would know how to take care of my baby and me, and she helped immensely. After she returned home, George and I took turns getting up during the night to feed Nevin, especially the first couple weeks while I regained my strength.

While attending Bible school each day and working evenings, George would get very tired and it was hard for him to stay awake while the bottle was being warmed on the stove. One night he brought the bottle back to bed and I began to feed Nevin. What he didn't realize was that he had left the pot of water on the stove with the burner still on. Shortly after, we heard what sounded like an explosion in the kitchen. We both jumped out of bed and raced to the kitchen to discover the water had boiled away and evidently, heat built up in the pot causing the bottom to crack. And, it was no ordinary aluminum pot; it was a heavy Club aluminum pot similar in thickness to an iron skillet. It and a larger one had been a wedding gift.

We felt it was very important to dedicate our son to God, because He was the one that had given Nevin to us. The school year would soon be over, so we asked the president, Dr. Milton Wells, if he would perform the ceremony. He was happy to oblige and scheduled it for a Sunday morning. It was a beautiful service and we were very grateful for his kindness.

Chapter 16

Our First Real Step Of Faith

B ible school was over a few weeks later and we moved to our first pastorate, which was located in a small village called Slate Run. It was nestled in the north central mountains of Pennsylvania in a place called The Pennsylvania Grand Canyon. It truly was a beautiful area with lovely mountains and a river that flowed through the valley. The road and railroad tracks followed the many curves that hugged the base of the mountains as it made its way through several small towns. It was a lovely place to live, but was almost 30 miles from a town of any size.

With no money to hire movers, we borrowed a truck and moved ourselves. While driving through that long valley on those winding roads and enjoying the beautiful scenery, a policeman pulled us over. We had no idea why he chose us, and when he asked to see our flares, we discovered we had none. We explained that we had borrowed the truck, and did not think to check it over for emergency items. He was very kind and allowed us to proceed to our destination with a warning! God is good! However, he did follow us to our new home, apparently just to make sure we had told him the truth!

Our first real home was in a building that housed both the parsonage and the church auditorium. There was no indoor plumbing, so George had to build our "outhouse."

There were poisonous snakes in those mountains, such as copperheads and rattlesnakes, so we had to be careful where we walked outside. Our time spent there was quite an adventure, and we learned a lot. It was also somewhat scary at times.

One day, I was out hanging up the laundry, when out of the corner of my eye, I saw something move on the ground. When I looked down, there was a snake and I let out a blood-curdling scream, which is unusual for me. George was working on the roof and scrambled down the ladder. He came running to see what had frightened me. I had heard if you saw one snake, there would be another one close by, so I wanted to know where it was! One never quite adjusts to all of God's creatures.

Chapter 17

Living By Faith

The Church Board promised us a salary of $15 per week, which was $10 less than what George earned working part-time at the furniture factory in Green Lane. Our "life of faith" was continuing, and we trusted God to meet our needs. He did not fail us then, and He never will!

Our home at Slate Run on Pine Creek was a bit primitive. Since there was no running water, our only source was a pitcher pump, but when it rained the water became muddy. So, we then carried water from a spring several miles from the house.

We never wasted water because it was a precious commodity. As we look back on those days, we wonder why we never thought to have the water tested to see if it was safe to drink, particularly with a small child in the house! God was looking out for us when we did not even realize it!

Nevin was two months old when we moved there, but when he was between 7 and 10 months old and not yet walking, he learned at that young age to be quiet and respectful in church. I had taken time to teach him to obediently sit still on my lap and not touch the keys while I played the piano, which we then repeated while I played hymns during church services. Surprisingly, he still remembers those early years and watching my hands bring music to life on the keyboard.

Since most of the men there had seasonal work cutting flagstone, it was not long until they could not give us the promised salary. The local store, which was a post office, grocery store and gas station all combined, offered credit to residents because of the seasonal work, but we determined never to charge anything.

One Monday morning after receiving no salary again, our food supply had diminished. We fed Nevin the last bit of morsels we could find in the house. During our devotions that morning, we asked our Wonderful Heavenly Father to come on the scene and meet the need.

God has promised in His Word to "supply all of our need according to His riches in glory by Christ Jesus." (Philippians 4:19) So, we just waited for God to take care of the situation.

It was not long until we heard a car horn blow outside the house. When we rushed outside, there was my father-in-law, mother-in-law, and our home Pastor, Rev. Oscar Byrd getting out of their vehicle. When they opened the trunk of the car, to our amazement, it was full of groceries! They had held a food shower for us at their church the day before, and also gave us an envelope with some money in it, and other gifts. Isn't it amazing how God always knows the need and sometimes answers and puts things in motion before we even pray?

George collects spring water.

Chapter 18

God's Hand of Protection

There was a small remodeling project that needed to be done on the church building, and had to be taken care of right away. George describes it here in his own words:

When God calls one into the ministry, it is not for a hundred yard dash, but it's a marathon race. We can quit, but God's Will is to finish the course He has planned for our lives. There were several times I was deeply discouraged, but God kept His hand of care upon our lives.

The remodeling job was to an old hunting camp cabin that served as a parsonage and church meeting hall. The church borrowed $150 from the bank and now with offerings low, could not meet payment on the loan.

When the work was finished and the final bill came, there was not enough money to pay it. I was embarrassed and ashamed about the situation and didn't know what to do. My pride would not let me ask the District Superintendent of the Assembly of God Churches for help and we personally did not have the money to cover the loan.

People may not realize the burdens often carried by pastors. Sitting in that mohair chair in our living room that night, I experienced God's hand of protection over one He had called into the ministry. When God calls, He keeps.

I Corinthians 10:13 assures us that if circumstances become seemingly unbearable, we will never be tempted above that which we are able to bear. God loves His servants, and keeps special watch over their lives.

God did provide and the financial need was met for this small remodeling project.

Chapter 19

A Tragedy Led To Our First Funeral

The railroad tracks ran right in front of our house, and each time the train approached a crossing, which was a short distance from us, the whistle blew extremely loud. Our first few nights there, we nearly jumped out of bed from fright, but eventually could sleep through that loud noise! It is amazing what you can adjust to when you have to!

Just after the train rumbled past our house one day, we heard a frantic knock at our door. It was our neighbor bringing terrible news. The Levin family attended our church and lived nearby. Their daughter, Thelma and her husband, were leaving their house and the car had been hit on the passenger side by the train. It had thrown their daughter completely out of the car and into the air. When she landed on the ground, the impact broke almost every bone in her body.

We jumped into the car and raced the short distance to the scene of the accident. We were about to face one of the most devastating experiences in our lives! Thelma had accepted Christ as her Savior, but her husband had not. When we arrived, Thelma was still conscience, which was unbelievable considering what she had just experienced. Her husband was nearby, but had not suffered injuries like she did, which had to be a miracle. Since Slate Run was about 30 miles from Jersey Shore, it took the ambulance approximately 45 minutes to arrive on those rural roads.

We felt so helpless, but tried to help Thelma all we could, and prayed that God would be with her and help her during this terrible ordeal, and to ease the pain she was suffering. Then I went to the house to be with her mother, who was caring for Thelma's five young children. How do you tell these little children that their mother had been involved in such a tragic accident and had been taken to the hospital? Her future was in God's hands, and for some reason, we learned later that day, He had seen fit to take her home to Heaven to be with Him.

There are times when we do not understand why tragedy comes into our lives, but we have to hold onto the fact that *God has a plan!*

Romans 8:28 And we know that all things work together for good to them that love God, to those who are the called according to His Purpose.

That was our first funeral service. It was a very difficult one, but God helped us to get through it! The Levin family was devastated for some time, but God was there for them as they leaned on Him and trusted Him each day for the comfort they needed so desperately! This was an unforgettable experience for a young pastor and his wife who had been in the ministry for such a short time.

Chapter 20

Fellowship And Friendship

We did not own a television set, and it didn't take a lot of activities to make us happy. In fact, taking a leisure ride up mountain roads was one of our favorite pastimes. It is hard to fully describe the beauty that was all around us, especially during summer months. There were all kinds of trees and beautiful wildflowers in the fields. Then in autumn, the vivid colors of fall leaves were spectacular. As days grew colder, leaves began to fall to the ground and crackled under our feet as we walked along. Wild animals could be seen quite often and deer seemed to be everywhere, especially during the early morning and late evening hours. It was also not unusual to see snakes warming themselves on the pavement.

There was one road on the mountain ridge lined with white birch trees, which was lovely to behold. You do not find beauty like that everywhere. Another such striking area of splendor that lingers in my mind is found in Savannah, Georgia, which we discovered years later. There, cypress trees with Spanish moss hanging from the branches make a beautiful canopy as they stretch across streets and intertwine one with another.

In those mountains, they had a very unusual annual event for their own entertainment. They had a "snake hunt contest." Prizes were given for the largest, the longest, etc. They put a huge wire cage in front of a store in one of the small towns. As individuals trapped a snake, they would bring it in and put it in that cage. You could not kill the snake; you had to capture it and bring it in alive.

Before that contest was over, there were so many snakes, that it was amazing they could find room for any more. They looked like they were all woven together as they slithered all around inside that cage! Not being one that cares for reptiles, I did not even enjoy looking at those creatures, and I am sure I was not the only one! However, that event did draw quite an audience!

Living in a small village in the mountains can also be very lonely at times. We met a minister and his wife in Jersey Shore, Pastor Fred and Esther Haddad, and we had good fellowship with them, which was very encouraging to us. They lived about 45 minutes away, but we met on different occasions and enjoyed the time we spent together. There are times when being in the ministry can make one feel very much alone. Ministers and their wives need friends they can count on because they have a tremendous responsibility, and most individuals do not realize its magnitude.

There is nothing like having good friends, and I do mean true friends who remain friends even when trials and tests come along.

We may not do everything right, and being human, we all make mistakes, even though our desire is to do the best we can under the circumstances. It has been said that during your lifetime, if you have five real friends, you are very fortunate. As I look back over the years of our lives, I know that has proven to be true. There were people that claimed to be our friends, but when things happened they disagreed with or did not understand, they turned their backs on us and made disparaging remarks that could put question marks in the minds of others.

The Bible has a lot to say about those who gossip, and especially the ones that claim to be Christians. We have learned it takes years to build up trust, but it only takes suspicion, not proof, to destroy it. May God help us never to be one that uses our tongue to destroy another child of God! We need to remember that God hears every word we speak, and He knows what is true and what is false. He also knows the intent of our hearts.

The word Christian means Christ-like. Stop for a moment and think what that really means! What is Christ really like, and what does He expect from us? The Bible says, "God will wipe away the tears from our eyes." Did you ever stop to think why we would be crying in Heaven? Do you suppose it will be because nothing is hidden from our Heavenly Father, and every harsh or unkind word we have spoken will be revealed?

When we utter innuendos instead of facts, we can cause someone's character to be discredited in the eyes of others. This often happens with people that feel very insecure, but they do not want anyone to know that fact about them. They are trying to make themselves look better in the eyes of others. It is like trying to climb the "ladder of success," but in order to do it, other people get stepped on and sometimes trampled in the process. That must truly hurt the heart of God.

In His Word, He tells us to love one another, and that means everyone, not just those who like the same things we do, or enjoy doing the same things we enjoy doing. I can remember how the tears flowed depicting the pain I felt when some of my "friends" made remarks that caused others to question my actions and integrity.

The Bible tells us in Galatians 5:14 and 15, For all the law is fulfilled in one word, even in this: Thou shalt love thy neighbor as thyself. But if ye bite and devour one another, take heed that ye be not consumed one of another.

Have you ever wondered if God sheds some tears when He looks down on this earth and sees the pain His children are suffering because of comments made by other members of the Family of God? The book of James is filled with admonition concerning the tongue… it seems it is almost impossible to tame. In fact, only God can do it—and only if we allow Him.

I realize none of us are perfect but we should strive to be, and we will make mistakes no matter how hard we try because we are human. Many times we may be misunderstood and misquoted; however, true friends can get together and talk things over and come up with a solution. We have found it takes hard work and a lot of understanding to be a true friend, but it definitely is worth the effort in the long run! A true friend is a treasure!

Chapter 21

Mid-West Revival

Most of the work in Slate Run was seasonal. It was not long until there was not enough money for a salary, so we moved to Jersey Shore. George acquired a job at Armor Leather Company, and we rented an apartment. We drove back and forth to Slate Run for the church services for a few months. It certainly was nice to have running water in the house, with a full bath! What a blessing!

There were less than 50 people in that small village and feeling we had accomplished all we could, we again packed up our belongings and moved. We felt God wanted us to return to evangelistic work once more, so we stored our furniture and went "on the road again."

Our travels took us back to El Dorado, Kansas for another revival meeting. This time, we took our car and loaded it with all the things needed for a small child. Nevin was almost a year old at the time and celebrated his first birthday while we were there.

The highways took us through many small towns and big cities along the way. It actually was a beautiful ride, but it took a lot longer to drive that distance than it would today. The trip went very well until one morning when we tried to start the car. It just sputtered a few times and would not do anything. Someone gave us a push, and finally it started. We made it to El Dorado that day, which was a very good thing because it probably would have never started again until it was repaired. Some of the valves had burned.

There was a mechanic who attended the church and said he would repair our car as his contribution to our ministry. We were so grateful because we did not have the money to have the work done. Once again, God came on the scene and provided for our need! It should not surprise me when God does those things, but it still is amazing! There is one thing we have learned through the years, and that is, when God leads us somewhere, He will always provide that which is needed; however, if we make our own plans, without consulting Him, then we had better be ready to cover the cost ourselves.

God did some powerful things during that revival meeting with souls being saved and homes rearranged, meaning homes in unity and harmony. Also, a miracle was performed one evening when a deaf ear was opened! God gets all the glory for everything that was accomplished! We were just the vessels God used at that time.

It was the same church we had ministered in the year before, and it was our privilege to return for another revival meeting. Quite a few of the same folks were still there, and it was our pleasure to see them again. However, after the service the first night, one of the ladies came up to my husband and said, "*You disappointed me this time.*" He was so shocked that he hardly knew how to respond to such a remark, but she quickly added, "*When you were here before, you always picked up the accordion for your wife, and helped her put it on, but this time, you just kept on talking, and let her do it all by herself!*" After he recovered from the shock, he smiled at her and they both had a good friendly laugh.

Chapter 22

Pastorate In Williamstown

We traveled back to Beckley, West Virginia and stopped to visit with Basil and LaVaughn. We enjoyed our time together there. Their pastor, who was my former pastor, Rev. Tommy Waldron, told us about a church in Williamstown that was without a pastor. Williamstown is a lovely small town nestled on the bank of the Ohio River. We went there and "tried out," and felt God would have us remain there to pastor their church.

The church was unable to provide a full time salary, so George took a job at the Fenton Art Glass Company in the shipping department. The company is a large producer of handmade colored glass in the U.S., celebrated 100 years in business in 2005, and is run today by the third and fourth generations of the Fenton family. They make some of the most beautiful glassware in the world, and tourists from all over the country walk through the factory to watch products being made, and to make purchases. Tours were very interesting and educational, and you could actually feel the heat radiating from those furnaces. The fire had to become extremely hot in order for the workers to mold the glass into an object of beauty.

It reminds me of some of the fiery trials we go through in this life. We do not understand why, but God wants us to yield to Him and be molded and shaped into the image He has planned for our lives. That is the only way we can truly please Him while we are on this earth. There are times when we are tempted to question God and ask why we must face these trials, but if we never have to walk through a valley and up the next mountain, we would never see the beauty that lies beyond. Each valley is meant to draw us closer to God, and help us become what He wants us to be. If we continually gripe about the problems in our lives, we will soon become "bitter" instead of "better."

In Psalms 23, God promises: In the valley, He restoreth my soul. I would like to encourage you to look at a valley as a growing time in your life, and it can change your whole outlook on trials and tests.

While at Williamstown, we heard about a young minister and his pregnant wife that had fallen on hard times and needed a place to live for a while. We lived in a two-story house at the time and did not have a lot, but were willing to share what we had with them. We did have an extra bedroom, so we invited them to come live with us for as long as they desired. We all got along great.

Williamstown is very picturesque with scenes like big barges making their way downriver. On the other side was Marietta, Ohio, which was much larger and where everyone did their shopping.

Our house was in a lovely neighborhood with a fire station just a few doors away. The fire whistle was extremely loud, and every time it sounded through the neighborhood, it startled Nevin and he cried. He was too young to understand what was going on, and I do not think he adjusted to that as long as we lived there. It was difficult for all of us, especially when the whistle blew in the middle of the night. It was heart wrenching to know the sound of that whistle could have meant someone somewhere might be suffering or lost to the Kingdom of God.

There were some wonderful people in that congregation, and we learned to love them very much. Years later we found out that one of the teenagers had been called into the ministry. We were thrilled to hear such a good report!

Chapter 23

Moving Again!

About a year or so later, we received a call and accepted a pastorate in Weston, West Virginia at a church with a lovely congregation. There was a parsonage next door that was in need of repair, and we did our best to fix it up. By this time, our salary had increased to a huge total of $55 per week in 1958. Even back then, it was difficult to live on that salary; however, God was good and provided for our needs day by day!

After we assumed the pastorate there, I had the privilege of learning to play the organ. I have always enjoyed playing the piano, but believe there is a time and place for organ music. It can be soothing to the soul.

The organ was in the sanctuary, so quite often I would go next door to the church to practice. The two keyboards were almost like playing the piano, but it took longer to master adding the bass pedals. After hours of practice, I finally had the courage to play in public. During the song service I would play the piano, and at the alter call I played the organ because it seemed more reverent during prayer time.

Summer was ending, and there were signs of autumn everywhere. Once again the hillsides were ablaze with a dazzling array of colors as leaves changed from green to brilliant shades of red, orange and golden yellow. Some views were breathtaking! God knew how much we would enjoy His artistic touch, so He took a brush in His hand and painted the hillsides once again.

My mother enjoyed traveling and it was a beautiful time of the year, so she decided to come to our home for a visit. She brought her mother, my Grandma Huffman, with her and we had a nice time together. It was a special joy to see my son have the opportunity to spend time with his grandmother and great grandmother.

Nevin was an energetic and inquisitive child and loved visiting with his two grandmothers. He even resisted afternoon naps and bedtime at night because he just didn't want to miss anything!

There was one humorous conversation that occurred while they visited that still lingers in my memory. They had stayed a few days and were planning to leave when an unexpected snowstorm developed. It was not a huge storm, but enough snow had fallen to make roads slippery, so they were unable to leave as planned. Grandma looked at my mother and said, "Gernie, I know George and Nadine might like comers and goers, but I don't know if they like comers and stayers." We all had a good laugh at her witty comment, including

Grandma. After a couple days, they were able to make the trip safely back to their home in Pennsylvania.

Grandma Huffman sure had an adventurous spirit! My cousin stopped by mother's house one afternoon where Grandma Huffman also lived and took her for a ride on his motorcycle. Even though she burned her leg getting off after they returned from a short ride, she said she would love to ride again sometime. She was a spry 82 years old when going for that ride!

Late autumn was usually the time churches would have revival services, which generally lasted one or two full weeks. Every time we invited evangelists to come to our church, they would always stay in the parsonage with us. We fed them and took care of their needs while they ministered to our congregation. The ladies in the church would make cakes and pies of all kinds, and bring them to our home. They were all delicious and we enjoyed them immensely, and I must admit they did not last long in our house!

There was one elderly lady by the name of Carrie Catlett, who was always concerned about our needs and wanted to make sure we had plenty of food for our guests. She always called to ask if we would come and pick her up so we could go to the grocery store. She would take a cart and walk down each aisle in the store and pick up every item she thought we might need in order to prepare all our meals. That was so sweet and thoughtful of her, and we did not want her to spend her hard earned money on us, but at the same time, we did not want to prevent her from receiving a blessing from God. She truly was blessed of the Lord, and God provided for her in a miraculous way throughout the remaining years of her life.

She not only blessed us, but there was a young lady in our congregation that wanted to attend Bible school but did not have the money to do so. One day, sweet Carrie came to us and asked George, "Pastor, what should I do? I know that Nancy is yearning to attend Bible school and really can't afford to go. I don't have the money, but I believe God would have me cash in my Life Insurance Policy so that I can pay her way. What do you think I should do?"

What a question! How many people would cash in an insurance policy to help someone else? My husband looked at her, and said, "Carrie, I really can't tell you what to do, but I will stand behind you in whatever decision you make." If God was laying this on her heart, how could George advise her otherwise? She truly felt that God was speaking to her, so she followed His leading and cashed it in and gave the money to Nancy.

Can you imagine how shocked yet thrilled Nancy was when Carrie handed that money to her, and told her to start preparing for the trip? She hardly knew what to say, and I am sure Carrie received the biggest bear hug in the world at that moment. Years later, we saw Carrie once again. She was living in a lovely personal care home and doing really well. She was a living testimony of God's richest blessings to an obedient child.

Chapter 24

Our Second Child Is Born

It was not long until warm winds were a thing of the past and there was an October chill in the air again. Right on schedule, the autumn leaves wilted and fell to the ground. With a small child in our home and another on the way, it was time to close windows and turn on the furnace.

When November arrived, snow would fall to be followed by children having snowball battles and going sled riding, as well as ending their outdoor winter activity with a traditional steaming cup of hot chocolate topped off with marshmallows. (This brings to mind a winter scene from a Christmas card.)

During a church service, I was playing the organ when I felt the first labor pain. I did not want to tell my husband, because I did not want to interrupt the service. So, when I had the chance, I sneaked out of church and on my way to the house, stopped to tell one of the ladies to come to the house if I did not return in a few minutes. It was not unusual for me to leave the service, because quite often nature called and I had to answer.

Our house being next door to the church made it very convenient for me, and it was only a matter of minutes until Maxine Slaughter came in the door. She stayed with me until the service was over. George, not knowing the situation, ended the service and actually drove the church bus to take people home.

When he arrived at the house, he was shocked to learn I had been waiting for him to come home so we could leave for the hospital. There was only one hospital in town, and it was privately owned; therefore, we had to take all the items the baby would need while we were there. It was most unusual, but we managed by packing two suitcases instead of one.

It was November 16, the day our second son, Craig LaRue, was born. This birth was much easier and the labor pains only lasted for 3 ½ hours. Craig weighed eight pounds and three ounces, and was a very healthy baby. He had a full head of dark hair, and it was not long until he had chubby cheeks, which people loved to pinch.

Right after I brought him home from the hospital, I did not feel strong enough to attend the mid-week church service, but living nearby, we could hear the music. Nevin, who was only 2½ years old, looked at me and said, "Come on mom, let's go, they are singing Bringing in the Sheets!" Children say the cutest things!

We had an experience there that was a challenge to our faith in God. After Craig was born, the weather was unseasonably warm so someone opened the window in my hospital room for some fresh air.

They forgot to close it, though, so it stayed open all night. The air cooled down and I slept in a draft.

A few days later after I had been discharged, I noticed something wrong with the left side of my face. I went to see the doctor, and he told me I had Bell's Palsy, and that I had probably obtained it by sleeping in a draft. A nerve in my face had been damaged, and was not reacting as it should, so that side of my face was paralyzed. The muscles did not respond to a frown or a smile, and my lips would not come together to form words correctly. I was heart-broken, and did not really know what to do. That was one of the most devastating trials I have ever faced, but I knew God was still on the throne and that He hears and answers prayer!

We had bought a movie camera to capture those special moments in the lives of our boys, but I always left the room when George picked it up, because I did not want my face to be seen on camera during that time.

There was no money to go to a specialist, so we just trusted God to do as he saw fit. The doctor said he would like to give me a series of B-12 shots, and maybe that would help. One day, I took Nevin with me for my appointment. He enjoyed going and was very inquisitive. After the doctor examined my face, he told me to wait there for a few minutes. Nevin wanted to know why we were waiting and I told him the doctor was going to give me a shot. His eyes grew wide with wonder and fright, and after looking all around the room, he asked, "Mom, where's the gun?"

God was good to us, and even though that nerve never completely healed, and all the muscles still do not respond, I did get better, for which I am grateful to the Lord.

A year or so later, we had another experience that was heartbreaking. The house where we lived had a furnace in the cellar, but instead of registers throughout the house, it had one large one in the center of the house.

We did not realize just how hot that register could get, until one day Craig tripped and fell on it. I quickly picked him up, but his arms had burn marks from his elbow to his wrist. Of course, he was in terrible pain, and we did everything we could think of to heal it. I would gladly have taken the pain for him, if it were possible! We could not get him to quit crying, so we took him for a ride in the car because we knew he loved to ride. We drove around for quite a while, and eventually he quit crying and fell asleep. However, he carried those scars for years to come.

After my dad had left our family in West Virginia, I did not see him very often, but he did stop by to see us a couple times. One time was in Williamstown when Nevin was very young, and the other in Weston, after Craig was born. Even though he had left us, I believe he still loved us. He just did not understand about being "born again," and evidently, he did not want to understand. It was not long after his last visit that we received word he had a massive heart attack and died almost instantly. He was only 52 years old. I was devastated, not only because I had lost my father, but because I was not sure if he had ever repented of his sins and accepted Christ as his personal Savior.

It was a very difficult funeral to attend, because we did not know if he had made his peace with God at the very end of his life here on this earth. No one should wait until the last minute to accept Christ as their Savior, because there may not be enough time or opportunity. It was also sad, because he would never get to know his grandsons.

Chapter 25

Resigning Again!

My sister, Dolores, met and married a wonderful Christian man named August Barnett, whom we all lovingly call Pop, a nickname he had since childhood. He was always very out-spoken about his love for the Lord, which was very refreshing. Some people seem to be ashamed to admit they are Christians, and it makes me wonder if God will be ashamed of them when they stand before Him someday!

On one of our visits to their home in Enola, Pennsylvania, we were told by their pastor, Rev. Paul Peck, that a nucleus of people wanted to start a new church in Marysville, which was nearby, and they needed a pastor. George told him we would pray about it and let him know.

The next week, we called Rev. Peck and told him that we had resigned our church and were planning to come to Marysville. We were shocked with his reply. He told us that another minister had already accepted that pastorate. Now, we had a dilemma of nowhere to go, and two children to think about! We had told the congregation in Weston that God was leading us out, so once again we needed direction from God.

On numerous occasions when we were in a pastorate, we would have a revival meeting and invite an evangelist to come to our church to preach. The services were wonderful with souls being saved and other miracles taking place. To God be all the Glory! One such evangelist was our good friend, Rev. Willie Tatum. By this time, he had stopped evangelizing, and he and his wife, Donna, had accepted a pastorate in Oldtown, Maryland. George called him to see if he would be interested in having us come for a revival meeting. He was very happy to oblige, and invited us to come as soon as possible.

God was good and blessed the services in a wonderful way. However, we did not know what we were going to do once this revival meeting ended. But, God knew, and had our future planned for us. We just had to wait on Him to direct our pathway.

One day the telephone rang and surprisingly enough, the man on the other end of the line, Marion Headlee, asked George if we would be interested in coming to Canonsburg, Pennsylvania to consider accepting a church there. It amazed us that he knew where we were, and how to reach us. George told him we would be happy to come the following Sunday. After arriving and ministering to the congregation, we felt it was God's Will for us to accept this pastorate.

It was 1961, and Nevin was about 5 years old at the time and Craig only 2½. We had taught our boys to sit still and reverence

God's House, but when they are that young, they were still in training, especially Craig.

When they heard one of us clear our throat, they knew that was the signal to sit down and be quiet. If that got no response, we then snapped our fingers, trying to be very discrete. If that did not change their behavior, they knew they were in trouble when they got home. To this day, if we are in a church service and I happen to clear my throat, Nevin quickly looks to see what I want!

Nevin loved music at an early age and had started to sing solos when he was three, and his diction was perfect. Everyone loved to hear him sing, and on the Sunday we "*tried out*" for the church in Canonsburg, he sang a song entitled "*He Washed My Eyes With Tears.*"

Since I was playing the piano, Craig was left alone on the front pew. Apparently tired of sitting, he started looking over the back of the pew at the people. George saw him and in his attempt to make a good impression on this congregation, gave the first signal of clearing his throat, and when that got no response from Craig, George snapped his fingers. Of course, Craig was so fascinated with looking at the members of the congregation that he paid no attention to his dad, but Nevin heard it. He looked back at his dad, saw the expression on his face, and just knew he had done something terribly wrong. Being very tenderhearted, tears welled up and began to roll down his checks. To everyone's surprise, he did not miss a word and finished the song. No one knew why he was really crying, except for us.

The church members voted on us, and it was almost unanimous. One of the women there, Mary Lou Thompson, used sign language to interpret the service for her deaf husband, Howard, and she was not sure about this man who talked so fast when he preached. She did not think she could keep up with him week after week. However, we soon became very good friends, and she did a wonderful job of interpreting, and eventually other deaf individuals started to attend the services. It was a wonderful sight to behold when they made their way to the altar to accept Christ as their Savior.

The building had comfortable and spacious rooms at the rear, which was our private residence. It was while we lived there that Nevin became old enough to start his education, and the elementary school was conveniently located right across the street. Nevin proved to be a very smart young man and quick learner.

We were invited to sing at an outdoor meeting one day, which was held in the yard of the Balentine family in Canonsburg. We gladly accepted the invitation and after singing a few songs, introduced Nevin. He was so little that we had to stand him on a chair so he could be seen. Everyone was amazed at how well he sang, and they enjoyed him very much. There was one lady that was especially impressed, and her name is Jean Treble. From that day forward, she became a part of our lives, and has been a faithful friend for many years. She has always prayed for us, no matter if we were nearby or far away, and I am sure she will continue to pray for us until the Lord takes her home to be with Him!

Chapter 26

A Trip To The Emergency Room

There were two incidents that happened in our Canonsburg home that could have had devastating results. Craig was about four years old when he followed his dad upstairs one day. While they were in one of the second floor rooms, Craig suddenly disappeared. After frantically searching for him, George discovered a section in one wall that seemed to open up. It appeared to be an old laundry chute no longer in use, but had been unsafely blocked off from future use. Craig had fallen through that space in the wall and landed in the room below. It caused us quite a scare! We thanked God he was not seriously hurt!

Another time, George's parents came to visit and everything was going well until Craig started running through the house and fell. The house was an older one with high baseboards and when he fell, he hit his head on one of the corners. It cut a big gash in his forehead, which caused the blood to flow. George was out visiting parishioners, so I had to call him to come home quickly so we could take Craig to the hospital.

When we reached the Emergency Room, they took him back to care for his injury. The medical staff could see we were in no condition to watch, so they asked us to go to the waiting room. Being so young, Craig wanted us with him and the last thing we heard as they took him away was, *"DADDY!"* Hearing a cry like that from our small child, knowing that we could not even be with him, caused indescribable pain in our *hearts*! It seemed like an eternity, but actually was not long until he was in our arms once again and we could console him. Thank God the cut was not life threatening and he would be alright, but it did require stitches!

The church grew and souls were saved, and we began to outgrow the church building. So, we made plans to build a new sanctuary. The day of the groundbreaking service was wonderful, and plans were in the making for our new church building. It was a very exciting time!

However, a few weeks later when we had a picnic on those grounds, my husband joined in the festivities and was playing baseball when he fell backwards and broke his wrist! George did not realize that day that it was broken, but that night he endured horrible pain. Of course, the end result was a cast that would stay on for at least six weeks. What a time we had, because he needed help with just about everything he did, including getting dressed. I know he felt helpless so many times, because there were things he just could not do for himself. However, we made it through that trial, also!

That summer, we heard on the news that President Kennedy had been shot in Texas! What a shock that was to our nation! It was hard to believe he was dead; in fact, it just did not seem to be real at all. However, death is real and each one of us will face it some day. The main thing that matters when we do face death is where we will spend eternity. There are only two places, and it is God's Will that we spend it in heaven with Him. However, the choice is up to each one of us. He leaves that decision in our hands, and our actions will show what choice we have made. If we choose Jesus Christ, His love will shine through us to others. If we do not choose Jesus Christ it will be reflected in our lives, and we definitely will not spend eternity in Heaven!

When the time came to start building the new church structure, the men decided we could save quite a bit of money by doing a lot of the work ourselves. Some worked in the evenings, but on Saturdays, you would see many men working on that building. The wives would prepare food and deliver it to the men so they would not have to quit work early to go home to eat. It was a joint effort and worked very well. There is a saying, "many hands make light work," and that is so true! The men were very appreciative for the good food, and we were very proud of their labor.

George spent many hours working on the building, and since he was a good carpenter, the work went smoothly and he accomplished quite a bit. However, he evidently was out in the sun too long one day and almost had a heat stroke, and, in fact, might have had one. We are not sure. But, thank God, he recovered rapidly.

Chapter 27

Our Third Son Is Born

One Saturday, it was my turn to prepare the meal and I turned on the oven and began to gather the ingredients needed to make meatloaf. After a few moments, I smelled a very strange odor. Looking toward the range, I saw smoke coming from the oven. Then I remembered, and exclaimed aloud, "Oh, no!" The week before, Wanda, one of our sweet friends from Cherry Valley, had brought us some wonderful homemade pastries in Tupperware containers. After we had emptied those containers, I stored them in the oven and was planning to return them to her on Sunday.

I quickly turned the oven off and opened the door. The sight reminded me of stalactites you see in caves, but this sight was a disaster because it was melting plastic! I cannot remember how long it took to clean up that mess. I think we had to buy some new racks for the oven! Tupperware is rather expensive and I wanted to replace those items, but Wanda would not even consider the matter.

It took months of hard labor, but eventually we were worshipping in our new sanctuary, and it was wonderful! We had plenty of room for Sunday School classes, offices and everything else we needed. God was so good to us!

The Pennsylvania Department of Transportation was building a new highway, so they bought our former church and property on South Central Avenue in Canonsburg. The building was to be torn down to make way for Interstate 79, so we had to look for another place to live. God blessed us by giving us the opportunity to rent a house in the Allison Plan housing development, which was only a few blocks from our new church building.

Summer ended and we felt the first cool air of autumn. Winter was just around the corner and as the air grew colder, snow began to fall covering everything with a beautiful white blanket. It makes everything so pretty and clean and sheets hanging on the clothesline do not look white next to snow. The Bible tells us that when we repent of our sins and accept Jesus as our Personal Savior, He will blot out our sins and we shall become as white as snow in His eyes! How wonderful is our God?!

It was a few weeks before Christmas when we learned that our family of four would become a family of five, but the new arrival would not show up until the following summer.

Our boys were taught they should always tell the truth, and they knew we would never lie to them. So, at Christmas time we told them the true meaning of the holiday. We read in the Bible, in the book of Luke, Chapter 2, where it gives details of Christ's birth and told the boys the reason for the celebration. We also told them that we buy gifts for them at Christmas time to celebrate the birth of our Savior.

One day we were in a store doing some shopping, and one of the clerks looked at Nevin and asked what Santa was bringing him for Christmas. He looked up at her, and said, "Santa isn't bringing me anything." She looked rather shocked, and then he said, "My parents buy my gifts." I am sure she was totally surprised at that answer, but that was alright. He had told her the truth!

It seemed that winter would never end. Finally, spring arrived and filled the air with the familiar fragrance of lilacs in bloom once again. As new life sprang up through the ground, barren trees brought forth new leaves, and flowers peeked through the soil, it reminded me of the new life I carried inside me. Would we be blessed with another boy, or would we have a girl this time? We didn't know, and didn't want to find out until the baby was born. As long as the infant was healthy, nothing else mattered.

By the time July rolled around, the temperature began to climb into the 80s; and believe me, I was very uncomfortable, being "great with child." There were times my feet were so swollen I could not wear shoes. I had to wear thongs to church, and did not feel dressed up at all! Of course, I went anyway, because I would not let a little thing like that keep me at home! I wanted everything that God had for me, and in church was a good place to receive it! We can miss out on many of God's blessings by not attending church services when the doors are open! Many individuals have excuses for not going to church, but I truly wonder how many of them are legitimate in God's sight! After all, His opinion is the only one that will count when we leave this earth and stand before The Judgment Seat of Christ!

The days passed by slowly, and it seemed July would last forever; however, the day for the birth of our third child was drawing near. We celebrated George's birthday on July 25, and just five days later our youngest son, Calvin Scot was born. He weighed ten pounds and six ounces, and needless to say, was the largest baby born in the hospital that day. When the time came for his feeding, all the nurses wanted to carry Scot, and argued over who would bring him to me. I guess they finally started taking turns!

As we looked into that sweet little innocent face, we just felt that he did not look like Calvin, so we decided to call him Scot. We don't even know why we felt that way, but he was called Scot for years. Then as an adult, most people called him Calvin, but he will always be Scot to us.

Libby Mitchell, who attended the church, offered to help me out for a couple days after Scot was born. George went to pick her up one day and as he opened the door to let her out of the car, two dogs that he did not recognize came running across our front lawn and met in mortal combat. They were snarling and biting each other. He slammed the door shut and told Libby to stay in the car. Then he proceeded to jump up onto the hood of the car and at one point jumped onto the roof and sat down to wait. They could not come into the house until the dogs quit fighting and walked away, which was sometime later.

There is a reason he was afraid of dogs, and that was because of a very bad experience when he was very young. His family was visiting relatives in the country when a dog came running after him. He jumped into Grandma Michael's arms just as the dog leaped toward him and caught its teeth in the seat of his pants! He came very close to having teeth marks in his flesh! The memory of an experience like that can stay with you for a lifetime!

The Van Riper family. From left are Craig, 5,
Nadine holding Scot, less than one year old,
George, and Nevin, 7.

Chapter 28

On The Road Again

Eventually, we felt the call to return to the evangelistic field. I think my husband had a stronger "call" to evangelistic work than to a pastorate, so I believe that is why we could not be content in one church very long.

We could not afford a motor home and it would be very complicated to travel with three children, so we had to make a very difficult decision and leave them behind with family and friends. Scot had become very close to a family in the church so he stayed with them for a while. Jim and Esther Gump, with their three daughters, Shirley, Bonnie and Judy, were just like family to him, so he was very content there. After a while, he was able to travel with us.

Nevin and Craig stayed with my mother because they had to attend school. She lived next to my sister, Dolores and her husband Pop, and the boys enjoyed playing with their three children, Gary, Teresa and Philip. Gary and Teresa were older than the boys by a few years and Philip was a few years younger than Craig, so they played well together.

There were times when we could go see them, and other times we had them come to be with us for a few days, which they enjoyed very much. In fact, one time we bought airline tickets so they could come to visit for a couple days. But, when they had to leave, it was very difficult. When we look back on those days, it leaves us feeling sad inside, because we missed out on so much of their lives in their early developing years when we could not be together. I still do not understand why it had to be that way, and even though we felt we were doing God's Will, we realize that being separated from our sons was probably one of the biggest mistakes of our lives.

Children are blessings from God, and there should have been a way they could be with us. I guess that is one thing I will have to talk to God about when I get to heaven. I'll ask the reasons, He'll tell me why, when we talk it over in the by and by. Later on, we told the boys how sorry we were for leaving them behind when we traveled!

Our travels took us to the southern states with revival meetings in various churches. It was so wonderful to see God work in the hearts and lives of individuals that would yield to Him. The most wonderful sight to behold is when someone will step forward to the altar to commit their life to Jesus Christ, by accepting Him as their Personal Savior and Lord.

Evangelists typically stayed in the home of pastors. When no space was available, they sometimes arranged accommodations in a motel. When that occurred, we sometimes received invitations into churchgoers homes for meals, sometimes breakfast and sometimes for the evening meal. Some seemed accustomed to entertaining guests while others seemed to extend the invitation for the first time. All were sincere and gracious, and I believe God blessed all for their generosity and willingness to be a blessing to a young evangelist and his wife.

One evening we were traveling through South Carolina and did not realize how low our gas gauge was getting until all of a sudden the car sputtered a few times and the engine died. We were in the swamps, and there was no town in sight. I don't know of a place that is darker than the swamps! We sat there for a while asking God what we should do. George did not want to leave me in the car and go for help, yet he did not want me to have to walk with him not knowing how far it would be to the next gas station.

That is when a car came by and a young service man stopped to see if he could help us. He sold us two gallons of gas, which was enough to take us to the next gas station. I think George gave him $5 for stopping to help us, which was a lot back then. You talk about God coming on the scene and providing. That is exactly what happened! I cannot imagine how long we could have sat there in the darkness had he not come along! No one can tell us that God does not care and that He does not provide for His children!

Chapter 29

Breaking The Ice

Our good friends, Pastor Don and Jean Arnold, invited us to minister in their church in Gadsden, Alabama. We were delighted at the invitation and arrived at their lovely home on Saturday night. They asked us to sing in the morning service and Pastor Arnold would then preach. Then, in the evening service, we would sing and George would preach. Their church could seat over 1,000 and that morning there were about 600 people in attendance.

At the time, George was a member of the Board of Directors for The Full Gospel Fellowship, and when it came time for us to sing on Sunday morning, Pastor Arnold gave us a most flamboyant introduction. We almost looked around to see whom he was talking about! The platform was the width of the auditorium and was about four feet high. When we were introduced, I went to the stairs on the left side and George took the middle stairs to the podium. When he had taken two or three steps, his foot slipped off the next step and he fell flat on his face. He was so embarrassed, but had to get up and step forward. Surprisingly, some parishioners thought he did it deliberately.

Then I started playing the piano and we sang together. When it came time for his solo, he forgot the words and just smiled and made up some of his own. We then finished the song and returned to our seats. After the service, a lady came up to him and told him she thought it was really cute how he made up some words to the song on purpose just to break the ice because it was our first time in that church. He told her he really had forgotten the words, and was not trying to break the ice. We all had a good laugh about it later.

Chapter 30

Drawn Back To Pennsylvania

Something happened in a country church in Illinois that was quite unique. My husband was singing the song, "He Touched Me," and when he came to the part that said, "Something, something happened…" he put his hand on the back of his neck, and said, "Something did happen," because he had been stung by a wasp! Usually, his neck would swell and become very red, but it did not even bother him. That had to be a touch from the Lord!

While we were ministering in Illinois, we were asked to "try out" for a church in Quincy. Everything went well and we were voted in to pastor their church with a congregation of around 200. There was a lovely ranch style parsonage, which we enjoyed very much. God blessed while we were there and the people were very good to us. We had wonderful services, and the Spirit of God worked in hearts and lives in a beautiful way.

It was while we were there that we had our first experience in producing a television program. We went to the television station each week to record a 30-minute program that would be aired the following Sunday morning. It seemed to be very well received in that area, and was something George thoroughly enjoyed doing. I was a little bit shy at first, but after a while, it became easier for me.

It was only a couple years later that God starting drawing us back to Pennsylvania. He laid it on our hearts to start a new church in Washington. It was not easy to give up a good salary and lovely home, and start all over again. However, if we want to please God and hear Him say, "Well done, thou good and faithful servant," we had better be ready to move when He says, "GO."

We had an adorable yellow parakeet with ruby eyes at the time, and enjoyed her so very much. Her name was Beauty, and we would occasionally take her out of her cage, and she would sit on our shoulder and talk to us. We could actually understand a few words that she had learned.

When the day came to pack up the moving truck, we let Beauty out of her cage for a while, because we knew she would be cooped up in a smaller cage for the long trip. She flew around and enjoyed the run of the house, until she landed on the kitchen floor. George did not see her and accidentally stepped on her, but as soon as he felt something under his foot, he quickly moved away. He stooped down and picked her up, but she laid very still in his hands. She did not move and didn't make a peep, so we didn't know if she would live or not.

Once we were in the car, I held her on my lap for hours, and she did not move at all. We thought her life was slipping away, but after a few hours, she began to stir and it was not long until she was chirping once again. It truly made us feel good to know she would be part of our family for a while longer.

Chapter 31

Soul's Harbor Lighthouse

We found a two-story house to rent in East Washington just at the edge of town and moved into it. We enjoyed living there and it was very accommodating for our family of five. We enrolled the boys in school and everything was going well. Living by faith had become a way of life to us; therefore, each week we trusted God for our needs and He always supplied.

One day I looked in the refrigerator and cupboards, and then told George we could use about $50 for some groceries, which at that time would buy enough to last all week. We told God about our needs—which He already knew, but He wants us to ask. He met the need that same day. When the mail arrived, there was a letter from a friend in Florida. He knew nothing about our financial needs, but had enclosed a check in the amount of $100, which was more than we needed. God is so faithful!

Another time God met our need in an unusual way was at the end of one month when we still needed $50 in order to have enough money to pay the rent, which would be due in a few days. The telephone rang and an elderly lady asked if George would come to pray for her because she was ill. He was happy to oblige and after prayer, he started to leave but she handed him a folded napkin, which seemed rather strange. When he got in the car, he unfolded the napkin and found a $50 bill! Was that a coincidence? No, that was God keeping His promises to us, and meeting our every need!

When you move into a city to start a brand new church, it takes a lot of faith and plenty of hard work. But, where God guides, God provides. We looked around for a building in which to hold services and found one downtown on East Beau Street that would seat about 40 people.

We named the church Soul's Harbor Lighthouse. It was a slow start, but eventually word spread around that a new church was in town, so it started filling up. Sometimes people came just to see what it was all about. Some liked what they heard and became a part of the congregation, while others just wanted to see what was going on and eventually went their way.

Over the years, I played music in our different pastorates and on occasion would play for weddings and funerals as George officiated. Most funeral directors hire an organist to provide music for their services; however, some of our church families would ask me to play instead. I felt honored to fulfill their requests. At times, I have been invited to fill in as pianist in churches where their regular musician could not fulfill their duty.

During our many years in the pastorate, we discovered there would always be some people who would come and go because they never wanted to commit themselves to be a vital part of a ministry. The comment has been made, "You can't build a church on rolling stones," and that is so very true. A church that thrives and continually grows is one that has a corps of individuals who will put their shoulders to the plow and do the work as unto the Lord. Some people do not attend church services because they expect everyone to be perfect, which will never happen.

The Bible tells us in The First Epistle of John, Chapter 2, verse 1, that we should not willfully sin; however, *"when we sin, we have an advocate with the Father, Jesus Christ the righteous."* So, all we have to do is ask Him to forgive us, and to help us to never make the same mistake again.

After about a year, our landlord told us he was selling the house we lived in and we had to move. We began our search for another rental. God provided another house on the same street just a few blocks away, and it was also a comfortable two-story house.

Winter was approaching, the temperatures were dropping, and snow began to fall. Craig was very industrious and had acquired a paper route. He was very faithful to his job, and was a trusted employee. However, one day he came home early and we could tell something was wrong. He was not usually afraid of dogs, but the one he had faced at one house was very large and for some reason very angry. When Craig turned to run from him, he hit his leg on a jagged piece of metal protruding from a parked car and knew he should come home to tell us what had happened. We could see he needed medical attention and should be taken to the Emergency Room.

Several inches of snow had fallen that day, and we could not even get our car out of the driveway. So, we had to call the police and they came with tire chains on the patrol car and drove us to the hospital. Of course, it takes time to see a doctor in the ER because they are always so busy. So, we spent our Thanksgiving Eve at the hospital.

Chapter 32

Meeting Our New Neighbor

We had not lived there very long until we discovered our next-door neighbor was an elderly lady named Tressa, who lived all alone in a three-story house. Other family members had lived with her, but all had passed away except a sister who was in a nursing home.

We went next door for a visit and found her to be a very sweet little lady, but also very lonesome. I cooked for my family every day, so quite often I would have one of the boys take a plate of food over to her, and she was so thrilled to have someone who cared enough to share with her.

With Christmas just around the corner, we asked Tressa if she would like to take a drive with us to see the colorful lights on display for the holiday season. She had not been out to see the gorgeous decorations for so many years, she was almost spellbound with the beauty of it all. We enjoyed sightseeing and talking together and when we arrived back home, invited Tressa in for some cake and ice cream.

Tressa was a little bit hard of hearing, so when George asked if she liked "hot tea," she responded with, "Yes, I like hog meat." The boys could not help but laugh out loud, and she just pleasantly laughed right along with them. She just enjoyed being with our family.

Knowing she was alone, we bought a little gift for her and it was under the Christmas tree. I guess she had not had a tree in her home for many years and had forgotten how beautiful they looked. She just sat in our living room staring at the festive tree with its keepsake ornaments and admired its delicate beauty.

When we gave her the gift, she could not believe it was for her. Tressa reacted like we had given her the most precious gift in the world. She was so grateful, I wondered how long it had been since anyone had given her a gift of any kind. It pleased us so much just to see that big smile on her face! She must have been lonely for many years, but she would not be anymore, not as long as we were around.

After Tressa's sister passed away, she began to be concerned about her own health. A local doctor lived in the house next to Tressa and checked on her physical condition from time to time.

Then one day, she came to the decision that Tressa could no longer live alone. We knew she did not want to go to a nursing home, so we invited her to come live with us. We made our den into a bedroom for her, and she was so thrilled.

She loved to eat, and was not hard to please. I usually cooked breakfast for the boys before they went to school, and Tressa would come to the table and eat with them. I think pancakes were her favorite, because she could keep up with the boys when it came to putting them away! That was hard to believe, because she was so tiny. But, it was wonderful that she had such a good appetite.

My sons made me proud because when they went to the cookie jar, they always asked Tressa if she would like to have one, too. Of course, she always did, and it pleased her so much that they would think of her.

A visiting nurse often came by to see to her physical needs, which was a great help to us; however, one day she found a problem that needed medical attention.

We were told she had to be moved to a facility that could care for her needs on a daily basis. The problem was cancer, and we felt so bad when they took her away from our home, but we felt even worse for her because she did not want to go. However, we could do nothing about it. It was very hard for her and it was not long until we received word that she had passed away. That was a difficult time, because she had become like family to us.

There was a humorous incident that happened while we lived there that still brings a smile to my face when I think about it.

There was a young man, John, and his girl friend Amy, who wanted to be married, so they asked George to perform the ceremony. It was a beautiful small wedding and they made a lovely couple. As it happened, they moved into an upstairs apartment next door to us, and they were very nice neighbors.

One warm sunny day, we had opened the windows and were enjoying the fresh air that flowed through the house. Craig had been disobedient, so his dad had sent him to his room. George was in the living room when he saw Craig sneaking down the stairs and said, *"You get right back up those steps."*

Right at that moment, Amy had come down her stairs and out onto the porch, which was only a few feet from our house. She stopped in mid-stride and looked all around, believing George was ordering her back upstairs. When we realized what had happened, we all had a good laugh about it!

The time came when we had to move again, and we located a house on Larch Street just a block away from the hospital. It was a lovely three-bedroom ranch style house, and it was so nice to have everything on one floor. There was a full basement, which allowed us to have a den as well as a laundry room. We lived there for ten years, and up to that point had never lived in one house that long.

One evening, we were watching the Andy Griffith Show as a family. It was the episode about an elderly gentleman who was being evicted from his home because he could not pay his taxes.

Among his belongings, though, they found an old bond, and it ended up that the town of Mayberry actually owed him a huge sum of money.

It would take quite a bit of figuring to know just how much that bond was worth. Scot, who enjoys mathematical challenges, took the time to calculate it all out and came up with 8.5 percent interest compounded annually!

Chapter 33

God's Protecting Hand

There were two times that God showed us how He was protecting us while we lived on Larch Street. The first occurred at 5:30 one morning when the telephone rang in the kitchen. This was before cordless phones, and we did not have a telephone in the bedroom. I went to answer it, and it was a man from our church telling us he had to take his wife to the hospital. I assured him we would be up to see her as soon as we could get there.

As I walked back through the living room, I noticed one of the windows was open. I looked around and also noticed the door leading out to the garage was open. Someone had broken into our home while we slept, and was ready to start carrying things out when the telephone rang and likely scared whoever it was away. Thank God for His perfect timing!

Another time, we had attended the evening service at church, and Scot and I came home because George always stayed to help close up the building and take care of some odds and ends there. It was dark when we reached our driveway, and as I glanced through the living room window, I saw the hall closet door was open. There was a light in that closet that only came on when you opened the door, and I knew I had closed it before we left.

Scot and I both thought someone could be in our house. He was still rather young, but pulled out his pocketknife and bravely said he would protect me. That was so courageous of him, and I was glad not to be alone! Of course, I had to go into the house to call George. When I walked in, I saw the back door was wide open, so I grabbed the telephone and quickly made the call. He told me to get out of the house in case someone was still there, but the thought crossed my mind that the intruder might have gone outside. I suggested that maybe we could just stay close to the door until he could get home, if that would be alright, so he agreed and hurried home.

The police came and dusted for fingerprints because there was evidence the intruder had been searching through the house. It appeared the main object was money, but we had very little cash in the house. Craig had a place where he was saving his change and had saved several dollars, but that container was nowhere to be found. In our bedroom, we had a few silver dollars in a drawer and they were gone. We thought nothing else had been taken, until we looked down in the den and discovered George's hunting rifles were also missing.

When we started pondering over the things that had been taken, we felt we had a pretty good idea who had stolen them. It would have to be someone who had been in our house, and had discovered where certain things were kept.

It was about six weeks prior to this time that George had met a young man at the City Mission, who told him he had no family and nowhere to live. We have always tried to help those who were less fortunate, so George brought John home with him and told him he could stay with us for a while until he could get a job and take care of himself. It soon became apparent he was not seriously seeking employment.

There were twin beds in Nevin's room, so John shared the room with him. One Friday night, George told John and Nevin that he wanted them to help him the next day with some work that needed to be done. Therefore, he wanted them to get up early and be ready, but the next morning when George was ready to go, he opened the bedroom door and John was still in bed. So, he told Nevin to stay there and keep an eye on John because he didn't know if he could trust him. He was unaware that John was awake, heard what was said and became very angry. John told Nevin later that he was mad enough to kill his dad and then left our house. Nevin did not tell anyone right away, because he thought John was just upset and saying things he did not really mean.

So, the next night when our house was broken into, Nevin and Craig had gone with some of their friends after the church service, but George called to tell them what had happened. The boys came right home because they were concerned for our safety, and especially for their dad, which Nevin explained further when they arrived. He conveyed what John had said the day before and suggested that his dad stay away from the windows, reasoning that if John had actually stolen the guns, he could easily make sure his threat.

We told the police about our suspicions, and when they located John, he had the guns in his possession. Therefore, they knew he was guilty. We did get the rifles back, but were saddened that Craig lost his money. John was arrested and George went to see him in jail. He asked him why he would rob us after we had befriended him. John claimed he did not know why.

It was some weeks later that a woman knocked on our door. When I opened it, she handed some silver dollars to me and explained that John was her son. He had gone home to visit and told her he had a job and the man was paying him with silver dollars. He wanted to know if she would exchange them for paper money. She did, but when she read about the robbery in the newspaper, she knew the money was ours and wanted to return it to us. We thanked her, but our hearts reached out to her because of her son's conduct. Parents are always affected by the actions of their children, whether good or bad!

This brings to mind an incident that occurred in church. A young couple, Gene and Ella, started attending our church, and one Sunday morning they walked down the aisle to the alter and accepted Christ as their Savior. Gene told his brother, Bob, about his experience and one Sunday he came to the service. Bob had never accepted Christ into his life and he listened intently to the sermon. But, when he heard George talking about sin in our lives, he was convinced that his brother had spoken to the pastor about his actions. That morning when the alter call was given, Bob, who was a very muscular man, got up from his seat and proceeded down the aisle. However, he was not coming to accept Christ, but was coming to knock the pastor out because he thought George was talking about him in his sermon.

When he was about halfway to the front of the auditorium, he stopped in his tracks as if frozen to the spot. The Spirit of God touched his heart and all of a sudden he realized he should accept Christ as his Savior. As George led him in the "sinner's prayer," his countenance actually changed and there appeared a "heavenly glow" around him as he became a "new creature in Christ Jesus." George had never seen anything like that before. Bob became a great friend and was a good supporter of the ministry for many years.

Chapter 34

On The Pittsburgh Airwaves

Radio Broadcasting always seemed to be a part of my husband's life, and the first program we ever hosted was in Weston, West Virginia. Years later, we had a radio broadcast on a station in Canonsburg, Pennsylvania. So, now we felt the need to secure a time slot on the WPIT Radio Station in Pittsburgh, Pennsylvania. It was a wonderful opportunity to spread the gospel of Jesus Christ and to invite people out to church services. George went to the station and talked with the manager, and they signed a contract.

There was a piano in the auditorium at our facility in Washington, so we had a telephone line brought in so we could broadcast with live music. We had taken some telephone calls, and prayed for requests on the air. We produced our first program and thought everything went well. However, the building did not have the best acoustics, and since our microphones were not top quality, the broadcast was not professional at all. We did not realize that until George talked with Station Manager Mike Komachek. When asked what he thought of the broadcast, Mr. Komachek said, "It was the worst program that I have ever heard. You were praying for kidneys and livers... it sounded like a butcher shop."

George was totally shocked and crushed because he had no idea the program did not come up to standard quality. He kept his composure, though, and learned a vitally important lesson that day. It was a blessing in disguise, because it showed us we should always use the best equipment and do the best job possible to present Jesus Christ to a dying world.

Soon the little storefront was filled to over-flowing, and we needed to find a larger auditorium. During our search, we noticed the Masonic Temple had a large auditorium with a baby grand piano on the platform, plus plenty of rooms that could be used for Sunday School classes. There was additional space for an office for George, and a room for the radio studio. We also had an office for the secretary, which made it just about perfect. God had opened the door to a facility that would provide for all the needs of our ministry. They were willing to rent the facilities to us, so we signed a contract and started to make plans for our first service.

We held services there on Saturday evening and Sunday morning for several years, and the congregation constantly grew from one week to the next. God blessed in such a wonderful way with souls being saved week after week, bodies healed, and homes rearranged. It truly was a Heaven-sent revival.

There is one lady that came one Saturday evening that I will never forget. Her name was Annabelle, and she had never been born again. She heard the salvation message and came to the altar to accept Christ as her personal Savior. It was so beautiful, and she knew that night that her life had been changed by the Power of God.

She came back on Sunday morning and told us she had painful arthritis and it was so bad that she had to take pills just to get going in the morning. Of course, she had to take more pills to keep going throughout the day. She heard us say God heals today, so she came forward for prayer. She came believing God would heal her, and He did. She no longer needed any of those pills because when God healed her, the pain left her body never to return! She was so thrilled she hardly knew what to do. She had a wonderful testimony and was thrilled to share what God had done for her with others.

Chapter 35

Christmas, A Time Of Giving

Shopping for gifts at Christmastime is something I really enjoy, and it was always a pleasure to see the excitement in our sons' eyes as they opened their treasures. However, one year with limited income, we had no extra money to spend on gifts and had determined never to buy gifts on credit. We did not mind for ourselves, but we did want our sons to have a nice Christmas with gifts placed neatly under the tree.

To us, Christmas is a time for giving and sharing with those less fortunate. Some people do not buy gifts for anyone. After living by faith all these years, we knew God would not fail us.

We needed a couple items from the store, so I went to pick them up. As I stood at the cash register, a long-time family friend came through the door. I looked up and we exchanged greetings and the next thing I knew, Bob came over to me and shook my hand and said, "One for you and one for the pastor." I felt something in my hand,

and when I looked down, I saw two $50 bills. Tears come to my eyes once again as I relate this story because when I got home, I showed George and asked him if I could use the money to buy gifts for the boys. He was in total agreement, and I felt so relieved knowing that our sons would have gifts under the tree that year after all!

After our sons had grown up and had families of their own, we always met together on Christmas Eve after attending a Candlelight Communion Service. Usually, we met at our house, had a bite to eat, exchanged gifts, and had a lovely evening together. It was always a special treat to read the "Christmas Story" from the Bible.

On one such evening, Craig had something he wanted to tell us, and in essence, this is what he said.

I think it would be really nice, if we as couples, would look around and find a needy family, and buy gifts for them so they can have an enjoyable Christmas. After all, giving is what it is all about, and we have plenty, but there are many who have almost nothing. How sad it would be for children if there were no gifts under the tree—if they have a tree. We all agreed, and it was not difficult to find needy people each year after that, which were totally surprised and elated to know that somebody cared for them.

Chapter 36

Camping Vacations

George always enjoyed the outdoors, so he decided to take the boys on a camping trip to Slate Run. I did not go along, because "roughing it" to me was being in a motel room with a black and white television! I have no desire to sleep on the ground in a tent in the woods!

They drove into the mountains, parked the car and found a nice little knoll just above Pine Creek. They pitched their tent and decided to see if the fish were biting. George had a permit to carry a pistol and had taken it along because there are dangerous animals in the mountains.

When one of the boys had a bite on his line, they thought it must be an enormous fish because it could hardly be reeled in. As he finally pulled it out of the water, they saw it was an eel. George grabbed his pistol and began to shoot; however, he did not take into consideration that there were stones everywhere around them and ricocheting bullets were the next concern. Thank God, no one was hurt!

One summer, I did agree to take a vacation with the family if we could rent a cottage. We found one just outside a small town called Weikert, which is in the central part of the state in Union County. We had to pack food, linens and everything else needed for a week. It would have been much nicer to stay in a motel and eat in restaurants, but our budget would not allow for that luxury. However, we enjoyed our time at that little cottage. It was many years ago, which means, cassette tapes had not even been heard of yet. We had a portable record player, so we took it along with some records and enjoyed sitting around a campfire at night, listening to good music, and roasting marshmallows.

George and the boys would go fishing, and I stayed at the cottage and cooked meals, did the dishes afterward, and swept the floor. It did not sound like much of a vacation for me, but it really was, because it was a change from our normally hectic schedule. We also had some good bonding time with our sons.

The bedrooms were upstairs, and one night we had some unexpected excitement! We had put the windows up, because the days would be nice and warm; however, at night it would cool down and actually get cold, so we had to close the windows.

In our room, the window was right behind the head of our bed, and instead of getting up and turning around to close the window, George decided just to reach up and pull the window down. But, it would not budge. So, he raised himself up just enough to put some weight on the window. It gave way and came down with a thud—on his thumbs. He pulled free, and then yelled because of the pain. He jumped out of bed and danced around the room holding onto his thumbs, which by this time were throbbing. When you are hurt like that, you know the pain will get worse before it gets better, and it did. The boys came running to see what the excitement was all about, and it took quite a while for things to settle down so we could all go back to sleep.

On another summer vacation, we took the boys to Cook Forest State Park at Cooksburg in northwestern Pennsylvania. The scenic 8,500-acre park is famous for its stands of old growth forest and has recreational and educational opportunities. The Clarion River runs along the eastern portion of the park and offers canoeing and rafting to see the natural wonders.

We rented a nice rustic cabin there and found things for the boys to do that they would enjoy. One day, they went horseback trail riding and had a great time. On their way back to the stables, though, Scot ended up on the ground because his saddle came loose and slid off the horse. It was rather comical, but at the same time scary for Scot, because he was pretty young at the time.

After enjoying several days together, we headed back home and plunged into our daily schedule. We took time to prepare for our regular church services, and there were always everyday chores waiting to be done.

Chapter 37

Expanding To Television

Our radio broadcasts were going very well and we eventually started a television program on Channel 7 in Wheeling, West Virginia, just a short 25-mile drive from our home in Pennsylvania. God blessed in a wonderful way and it was not long until an agent from Virginia contacted us about expanding to other stations. He had plenty of contacts, so pretty soon we were broadcasting on 15 radio stations throughout the U.S. and four television stations. That was quite a load to carry, but God gave us strength to keep going. By this time, our congregation, which consisted of many families, had grown to about 350 in attendance.

We saw the need for training Christian workers, so we started Bible School classes and had a wonderful group of qualified teachers. We bought a house, which served as a dormitory for students, and members of our congregation volunteered to cook meals for them. Students came from several different states and as they applied themselves, did very well. Our one big mistake was not hiring a principal. George was pastor, principal and a dean, and you just cannot be a good spiritual leader and serve as a disciplinarian as well. That can lead to serious problems, and it did!

So even though things seemed to be going great and God was meeting needs, Satan began to cause an undercurrent. Isn't it amazing how the devil can cause God's children to be blind-sighted, and use them to cause division among the body of Christ?

When we read Proverbs 6:16–19, we can see what God has to say about such things! It is an abomination unto God, to sow discord among the brethren, and it makes no difference as to who is right and who is wrong.

We received a telephone call one day and found out that a man in town had made a threat on George's life. The man was very upset with Nevin and was going to get even by killing his dad. It was reported he would be coming to our Saturday evening service to make good his threat. It just so happened that a police officer attended our church and when George told him about the telephone call, he told the Pastor not to worry because he knew the man and should he walk through that door, he would handle the situation.

Thank God, the man did not show up because that would have certainly disrupted the service, which we did not want to happen. Maybe he was just blowing off steam when he made the threat, but we were so grateful for God's Protection.

Chapter 38

Trip To A Foreign Land!

W e had never traveled outside the United States, but during 1976, God was leading us on a path to travel to India. So, we began making plans to take a missionary trip there. We did not have the necessary funds to make the trip, but knew God would work it all out since He was the one directing our pathway!

Airfare to India back then was approximately $1,000 each. We mentioned on the radio broadcast that if anyone would care to make a small contribution toward the trip, we would bring back a small gift for them. The elephant pictured at the beginning of this chapter is one beautifully carved from Rosewood, an important timber tree in India, which we brought home for my niece.

Time was passing by and the scheduled trip was just a couple months away. Only about half of the needed funds had come in, which caused a little concern. There were quite a few inoculations required before we could make the trip, not to get into India, but in order to be allowed back into the United States! Even before all the necessary funds were in our hands, we knew God had a plan and that we were going. So, we kept getting the required shots and trusted God to come through for us one more time.

For some reason, which I no longer recall, we decided to change our checking account to another bank and wanted to take care of the matter before our trip, which I remind you was in God's plan. So, with checkbook in hand, we went to the bank.

We told the clerk we were closing our account, and that we wanted to write a check for the remaining balance. I have always been very meticulous about keeping the checkbook in order and accurate, and if my memory serves me correctly, we only had $167.45 in the account. When I quoted that amount to the teller, she checked the records and said, "Wait a minute. Don't write that check yet because our records show a balance of $1, 167.45." We told her it was impossible for that much money to be in our account and claimed there must be a mistake.

She checked again and told us we should make the check out for $1,167.45. We emphasized that we could not take that money knowing it was not ours, but she insisted the bank could not keep it because our account showed that balance. After some extensive searching, neither of us could find out how that money was placed in our account, and it still remains a mystery today. However, we do know it was God's plan for us to go to India, so we give Him all the credit!

That is how God supplied the remaining necessary funds for us to make a missionary trip to India! Was it a miracle? YES! It was! Nobody can tell me that God is not a Miracle-Working God!

Our trip would consist of about 28 days, so there was much to be done before we could leave. There were television and radio broadcasts to be pre-recorded, plus many other things that needed our attention. For instance, we had to make the necessary arrangement for someone to fill the pulpit at our church while we were away, and also a musician to help with the song service. After much work, planning, and prayer, everything was in place and we felt free to go.

Nevin was attending Bible school then and living at the dorm. Craig and Scot were still living at home and we needed someone to be there for them. One of the married couples that was attending Bible school, David and Carol Brown, volunteered to stay in our home with the boys, which was such a blessing to us.

Tom and Bonnie Gilbert attended the Soul's Harbor Lighthouse Church, and they were a tremendous help to us in planning our flights and making reservations at a hotel in Bombay. She was a travel agent and he worked for U.S. Airlines. At the time, we had no clue what affect this missionary trip would have on our lives, and that we would never be the same again.

Another couple, Dave and Sandy Ross, who were also members of the Soul's Harbor Lighthouse Church, decided to make the trip with us. That was good news, because it was nice to have familiar friendly faces around us when in a foreign country, and a lot of times, we were the only Caucasians in the area.

Our flight from Pittsburgh, Pennsylvania to Bombay, India took approximately 20 hours. The airplane was a Boeing 757 and there were quite a few empty seats. When the movie came on, which was entitled, "Jaws," we decided it was time to go to sleep. After all, it was our bedtime, and we did not want to watch a movie about a man-eating shark as we flew across the ocean! We could not believe their choice of movies when there were plenty others that would have been very entertaining and wholesome!

Landing in Bombay was quite an experience because most of the people there thought all Americans were rich. Some parents would bring their children to the airport so they could carry luggage for travelers, which would earn them a few rupees.

Going through customs for the first time was another experience, and naturally they looked through our entire luggage. Having a sweet tooth, we had taken some candy bars with us and they were packed away in our suitcase. When they saw them, they told us candy bars were not allowed, so they confiscated them. I think they just wanted them because they came from America, so we did not say anything and just let them have the candy.

We had made advance reservations, so after arriving at the hotel and checking in, we ventured outside for a walk and were immediately faced with beggars. We felt compassion toward these people and wanted to help them, but there were so many we could not afford to give money to all of them.

That evening, we again went outside to explore the area. Right in front of the hotel was a man playing an instrument very similar to our flute, and there was a basket sitting right in front of him. We paused to listen for a few moments, and were shocked to see a cobra suddenly lift its head up out of the basket. Its head swayed back and forth with the music, and I must say that it was a scary sight.

Normally, when the "show" was almost over, the man would allow a mongoose to kill the cobra. However, this man had a black snake in a bag and allowed the mongoose to kill it instead. I guess he knew he would have to catch another cobra before he could present another "show" for his income. So, he put the lid back on the basket to keep the cobra inside. There were quite a few people that gathered to watch, and some rewarded him with a few rupees, which is comparable to the change usually carried in our pockets.

That night when we went to our room, which was on the seventh floor if my memory serves me correctly, we looked out the window into the dark night. We could see individuals on the flat roofs of their houses. They had built a fire and were kneeling to pray to one of their countless gods. It seems amazing that these people would pray night after night to a god that I believe could not even hear them. We were not allowed to enter their temples, but were told they do have a picture of Jesus inside.

The next morning we flew to Trivandrum in southwestern India to meet with missionary Rev. Earl Stubbs who invited us to come for revival services. They lived in a very modest home on the grounds of a Bible School in Punalur in the state of Kerala. The climate was very warm, so there was no need for a jacket or even long sleeves.

There was no running water in the house so when we took a shower, we carried the water in from a well. There was a small area just inside the house where we could soap up and rinse off by pouring water on ourselves from a pitcher. The water disappeared down a drain. So, it was a good thing the temperature was very warm, because the water was very cold!

The missionaries had a native cook named James. He could actually cook "western style," which was wonderful because just about all food in India is highly seasoned and very spicy. They often use curry, which will heat your pallet very quickly. Years later, one church official and his wife came to our home in Washington, Pennsylvania, and they wanted Tabasco Sauce on just about everything I cooked. I did not mind because I knew our food would taste rather bland to them because it was not highly seasoned.

The missionary scheduled quite a few services for us while we were in India, and we felt it a privilege to sing and preach many times. I have never seen people with such a hunger to hear gospel music and the preaching of God's Word. I could not begin to tell you how many souls were saved during those services. We did not want to keep track, because God gets all of the glory for what was accomplished during our stay in that foreign land. We were just happy to be the vessels He chose to use at that time.

Chapter 39

Miracle During A Sermon

We then traveled to nearby Ernakulam, Cochin and held services in a vacant lot in the middle of the city. During previous services, people sat on the ground. At these meetings, they had chairs. Something happened there that we will always remember. After some singing, they asked George to preach. No one had told him how to work with an interpreter and during that first service, he thought he should just say a few words at a time, not realizing that Philip needed a whole thought before he could interpret. It was not flowing like it should have been, and George was becoming frustrated but kept plugging along.

There were several ministers there seated on a porch right behind the platform. I don't know how many people were in attendance that night, but I believe there were several hundred. They were so hungry for the Word of God and were so very attentive, even though their P. A. system was of poor quality. George did not see a lady coming toward the platform carrying a baby, but he did notice the ministers all went into the house. He could then hear them praying loudly and earnestly. He thought to himself, oh, no, I am doing such a terrible job that they had to go inside to pray for me. After several minutes of intense prayer, they came back to the platform for the remainder of the service.

George just kept on preaching but it was a struggle. Finally, the missionary walked up behind him and told him to finish a complete thought before pausing to allow Philip to interpret. He was so embarrassed but it was a learning experience and everything went smoothly after that night.

Afterward, the missionary told us the baby had died during the service, so the mother brought the child to the ministers and asked them to pray. They went inside and prayed for the baby and God brought the child back to life! Can you imagine the Praise and Thanksgiving that went up to God's throne that night? Faith in God can bring miracles to pass, and this was one of those miracles! We ministered in that city for several nights, and there were numerous individuals that accepted Christ each night.

I must explain here that about a year before that trip, God had given George a vision that he would be preaching in another country through an interpreter. We didn't know when that would occur, but when Rev. Earl Stubbs invited us to come to India, we knew God had spoken. The vision had come to pass because we did need an interpreter for the preaching. Philip was definitely used of God, and after that first night, he did an incredible job. Many people responded to the altar call and found Christ during those services.

One man in particular stood out to us. He was a very distinguished looking gentleman, and very sincere as he accepted Christ as his Savior. We noticed he did not return the next night or the next, and wondered about him. The missionary told us he could have been a Hindu, in which case, his family may have killed him or he may have fled for his life. We never did know what happened to him, but we thank God we knew where he would spend eternity.

The new converts wanted to be baptized, so we met early on Sunday morning by the riverside and held the service. It was beautiful but at the same time very strange, because in the same river, we could see people bathing, washing their clothes, brushing their teeth, and some were bathing their bullocks! What an unusual sight that was for us!

One Sunday morning, communion was served and everyone drank from the same cup. However, Rev. Stubbs told us we would be served with a cup of our own, which Dave, Sandy and I drank from, but George wanted to share the cup with the people there, so he did. He was taking a risk, but God protected him, for which we were very grateful!

Chapter 40

The Orphanage

There was an orphanage a few miles away, and each evening a group of young people and adults came to the services. They walked to and from the meetings each night. That might not sound unusual, but at night poisonous snakes would be on the pathway and they had to be careful, so they carried flashlights. They wanted to be there and attended every evening, regardless of the danger they would no doubt face during the long walk home after dark.

Rev. Stubbs told us about a lady who started an orphanage and was taking care of little children that needed a home. So, one day we went to visit her. When we knocked on the door, no one answered but we heard someone calling out to us. The voice said, "Come on in and I will be with you in a few minutes." We thought that was very strange, but we walked inside and waited. Several minutes later, an English lady walked into the room with a baby in her arms. Someone had left the infant on her doorstep and she had been bathing and dressing it when we arrived. She was very business like, but made us feel welcome. Her name was Ms. Edith Greet. She had never married, but had come from England and cared for abandoned children for many years. They had become her family and she loved them dearly.

On the flight there, God spoke to George's heart concerning helping with a project in the land of India. He was not quite sure what God wanted, but felt it had something to do with an orphanage, so he kept his heart open and waited for God's guidance. Ms. Greet took us on a tour of the orphanage, and was very proud of "her children" and their home.

There appeared to be several repairs that needed to be taken care of, and before we left, George asked her what was needed the most. She did not get all excited because many people had come before and offered help, but they went home and forgot all about their promise. She did say they needed a new tin roof on the porch where they dried clothes on laundry day. George asked her what the cost would be and then told her we would send a check for that amount shortly after we returned home.

When she later received our letter with the promised check inside, she was thrilled and surprised all at the same time. She wrote to us and told us that she was so grateful we had remembered, and had kept our promise. At that time, she did not know she would be receiving a check each month for years to come to help with her wonderful ministry. That experience developed into a good relationship that has lasted for many years.

She has come to America on several different occasions, and stayed in our home as well as others who invited her. She is one woman that truly sets an example of being obedient to God and doing His Will all of her life. She is elderly now, and probably will never get back to the states again, but we will definitely meet in heaven some day! I am sure her crown will be covered with many jewels because of the tremendous sacrifices she made during her many years in that deprived country.

We rode with another minister to one of our meetings, and that ride was quite exciting for us. We thought he was driving too fast for conditions, and he did not appear to be a good driver and we wondered why. As we rounded a bend, there was a large herd of bullocks in the middle of the road, and all he did was blow the horn over and over again. Finally, they meandered off the road and we could be on our way. Later, we found out he had been driving only a short while!

Sometimes during the daytime, we would walk through the city and check out the stores. It seemed like every clerk wanted to sell us something. Like I said, they think all Americans are rich! We had very little money over and above our expenses, so we could not buy very much, but we did manage to bring home a few souvenirs, which were appreciated. Each clerk would tell us the price of the item, and then expected us to barter. That was something we had never done, and did not really want to do, but we finally settled on a price.

That day, Philip, our interpreter, and his wife, Leelamma, were with us. After we made our purchases, she quickly picked them up to carry them. Being the gentleman that he is, George reached out to take the packages from her, but Rev. Stubbs stopped him and said the custom is for the women to carry the packages, and walk behind the men. That was probably one of the hardest things George ever had to do, but he did not want to offend her, which he would have done if he had taken those packages from her.

When we went to the city to hold a revival meeting, we stayed in an apartment with the missionary and his wife. We met a minister and his wife who lived next-door, Rev. Johnson and Annamma. One morning, George went out on the veranda and she was outside sweeping her porch. He wanted to be friendly and say something to her, so he tried to call her by name. Evidently he mispronounced it, because she just snickered and went into the house. George told the missionary what he had said, and found out that he had just called the lady an elephant! In that country, an emphasis on the wrong syllable can totally change one word into another. She was very nice about it, though, because she knew what he was trying to say.

One day, we strolled along in the sand by the Indian Ocean, and the color of the water was a beautiful shade of blue. It was a lovely day, and the ocean breeze was very invigorating. We were never alone, though, because everywhere we went, there were people that followed us. Maybe a lot of them had never seen white people before, and that would make us a novelty to them.

As we walked along the roads, it was very interesting to observe people at their craft. Some were gathering rice in the fields and would earn enough to feed their family that evening. Others were sitting by the wayside making hair combs out of ivory. Using their feet to brace a piece of ivory left their hands free to carve out teeth, one by one. It was a tedious and time-consuming process to create just one comb, but when finished, these sought after exquisite combs would last a lifetime.

There were some beautiful sights and some sad sights that we saw while in that underprivileged country. One day, we saw a mother carrying a small child while she looked through a garbage can to find something for them to eat. It must have not been unusual, because no one else seemed to notice. There were also very many people who were crippled or deformed, and it was heartbreaking to see their condition.

Rev. Stubbs took us to meet the president of their bank. When we arrived, he was very cordial and gracious and ordered some tea to be brought into his office. Up to this point, we had not been served tea so we did not know what to expect. It was dark in color, very sweet, and thick like syrup. I must say that I had never tasted anything like it. We did not want to be discourteous, so we drank it and thanked him for his kindness.

One day we went to the market in town, and when we came to the place where they were selling fish, the odor was so bad we could not go inside. Dave took a deep breath, ran in, took a snap shot, and hurried back out before he took another breath. Then we saw some beef they were selling, and it was all covered with flies and bugs. No wonder there is so much sickness and disease in that country.

It was not long after we left the missionary's house on the compound that they called in the snake charmers to capture poisonous snakes and remove them from the grounds. This had to be done time and time again, because there were so many reptiles in that area. One day, they captured 26 cobras. It is amazing that we did not see them while we were there, and it was probably a good thing, too!

Our time there caused us to have experiences we will forever remember, and we are so glad God chose us to make that trip. We were thrilled to see the many souls that came to know Jesus during our stay, and also the other miracles that took place in answer to prayer when faith reached up to God.

The day of our departure was fast approaching, and it was time to fly back to the United States. Seeing the poverty in that country changed our lives completely, and we came home totally different than when we left. Months later, it was still very difficult to go out and buy a hamburger in consideration of knowing what even that small amount of money would do for just one person in India.

We quickly learned that while we ministered in India, Satan had been working overtime back home and things were in disarray. The finances that had come in were not sufficient to cover the cost of broadcasting on television and radio, so we had to make some serious decisions. After going to India and seeing the sacrifices people made just to be able to attend church services there, and then coming home to see how people had allowed the enemy to deceive them, was very depressing. George became very discouraged, called the television stations, and cancelled our telecasts. We did not even have a chance to let our audience know why we had to curtail our television shows. Somehow, we managed to keep the radio broadcasts on the air for a while, but eventually they were cancelled, too.

Chapter 41

A Time For Grief

God worked out perfect timing for our missionary trip, because we had been home only a few days when we received a telephone call informing us that my mother-in-law was in the hospital and very ill. We quickly packed a couple bags, took our three sons, and drove to the center of the state.

We went straight to the Lewisburg Evangelical Hospital, and when we walked into her room, realized she would soon make her journey to heaven. The doctor told the family she had a strong heart but was tired and weary, and her desire was to go to her eternal home. Therefore, she would not be with us much longer.

It was Saturday, and we needed to return home for our Sunday worship services, so we told our family to keep us informed. On Sunday afternoon, the telephone rang and we were told that Mom did not have long to live. Therefore, as soon as the evening service was over, we jumped in the car and headed back to Lewisburg. It took us a little over four hours to make the trip, and it seemed as though she was waiting to say goodbye to each of her children. We had not been there very long when she went "home." She was sorely missed by family and friends.

She had written out plans for her funeral service including the clothes she wanted to wear. She wanted us to sing a song entitled, "How Great Thou Art." With God's help we were able to get through it. It was a tough time for the family, but God is always faithful to give comfort to His children when they reach out to Him. After the service, we traveled back home with saddened hearts.

Chapter 42

The Wedding That Almost Was

Years later, while talking to my mother on the telephone, she told me she had some news for me. I could not imagine what it could be, and was totally surprised when she explained she and my father-in-law had been dating and were planning to be married. It was almost funny, but at the same time, I could see where it would be nice for her to have some companionship. My dad had passed away many years ago, and my mother-in-law had been gone for several years also.

My mother wanted a church wedding this time because she did not have one before. She called me one day to ask if I would come to help her make wedding gowns.

I had made my first dress while in home economics class in high school. Years later, I sewed my own dresses, suits, full-length gowns, and even made matching vests for our young sons. With a limited budget, it was much more cost-effective to make clothing.

So I went, and we spent hours making beautiful dresses. She even made her own gown, and it was gorgeous.

As the wedding date drew near, though, she became less excited about the event. Then she considered calling off the wedding because she just did not feel right about it. When we have doubts, we need to stop and weigh our options, and make the right choice. So, the wedding was cancelled. She never did remarry; however, my father-in-law did and seemed to be quite happy. When we look back on it, I see that everything worked out just fine.

Chapter 43

Following God's Will

W e ministered in various churches of large and small congregations and sometimes the free-will offerings did not even cover our expenses of transportation but we continued to follow God's Will.

This occurred at one particular church about a two-hour drive from our home. The service went well and there was wonderful fellowship, but George became very discouraged on the ride home after we discovered the free-will offering presented to us created an unfortunate financial situation and did not cover our expenses. I said, *"Honey, there must be a reason for what happened, and I know that God will make it up to us at another time and another place."* He thought about that for a few minutes and agreed. Little did we know how soon that would come to pass.

A few days later, we received a call and invitation to minister in a coffee house at Wheeling, West Virginia. The man in charge,

John, is a chiropractor. He is not a pastor, but a Bible teacher. He taught a small group there each week. We, of course, went and had a wonderful service together.

The next Sunday night, they came to our church service and God blessed in a fantastic way. In fact, that was the night our son, Scot, was filled with the Holy Spirit. At the conclusion of the service, George asked John to come to the platform and say the closing prayer. John asked if he could say something first, which was fine. He turned to George and asked, *"What do you need?"* Of course, the first thing on George's mind was the ministry. But John said, *"No, I mean what do you personally need?"* He thought John was going to agree with us in prayer that God would provide for our need. So, he told him that our car had high mileage on it, but we could not afford a new one.

Then, what he said to us was a shock and thrill all at the same time! He said, *"Go shopping and pick out any car that you want, and we are going to buy it for you. God laid this on my heart during the church service."* We were so stunned we did not know what to say, for nothing like this had ever happened to us before.

His wife came up to me and told me they were leaving for Florida in a few days, and would spend the upcoming holidays there, adding that we should go pick out our car within the week. Before Christmas, we were driving a brand new 1982 navy blue Oldsmobile 98. Now, you tell me, did God make up for that night of discouragement, or not! I feel He made it up a thousand times over!

It wasn't long before we made our first trip with our new vehicle. George is a member of The Full Gospel Fellowship, and was a board member for several years. Each January, the Board would get together for a few days in order to plan the next International Conference. Since God had so wonderfully provided us with a brand new diesel Oldsmobile, we decided we would drive to our meeting and invited Pastor Henry and Betty Howells to ride with us. They only lived about an hour away, and he was a board member, too.

We needed to leave on Sunday afternoon in order to arrive at Kansas City in time for the scheduled meetings. Henry and Betty drove to our house on Sunday after church and we ate lunch together. Then we loaded the car and left. It was a bitter cold day, but the car was nice and warm and we were enjoying the trip. After a few hours of driving on Interstate 70, we had traveled through the West Virginia panhandle, and were in Ohio when George asked Henry if he would like to drive for a while. It was not long after that when the car began to slow down, even though he tried to keep up to the speed limit.

He asked, "George, what's wrong with the car? It just keeps going slower all the time." Betty and I were in the back seat and began to pray that we could reach a service station. It was entirely too cold for anyone to have to walk for help should the car quit on us. We came to an exit, and found a station nearby. Of course, we stopped and George went inside to see if anyone there could be of help to us. Since it was Sunday evening, none of the repair shops were open, and there were no mechanics in sight.

The man who owned the station introduced George to his father-in-law, who was the sheriff. He told us we would have to leave our car there at the station, and he would drive us to a motel for the night. Then we could call the Oldsmobile dealership on Monday morning, and they would tow our car in and see what the problem could be.

We grabbed a couple suitcases out of the trunk, and piled into his car. There was a very small town nearby, so the choice of motels looked very bleak. He drove a few miles and dropped us off at a small motel. As it turned out, there was only one room available and we would have to share. We had never shared a room with anyone else before, but we had to stay somewhere so we made the best of the situation. There were two beds in the room, but only one pillow on each bed, so we had to share that, too. We took turns going into the bathroom to dress for bed. We then sat on the bed and played a game of Uno and laughed at our situation, which was better than complaining.

Why not laugh? The Bible tells us that "a merry heart doeth good like a medicine." So we were well medicated that night! If our church members could have only seen us then! Of course, we had no control over the situation. We did not sleep well but when morning finally came, we dressed and went out to the small restaurant adjoining the motel. We only had a few snacks for our evening meal the night before so, needless to say, we were hungry!

We were given a ride to the nearest Oldsmobile dealership, and they towed our car in and located the problem. There is an additive that must be used with diesel fuel when the temperatures are extremely cold, or the fuel will gel and not circulate properly. Thus, the line gets clogged up, and the car will not function in a normal way. It would take hours for the mechanic to get it back on the road again, and if we waited, we would be late for the board meetings.

Our only solution would be to check the airlines to see if we could get a flight out of Columbus. It is amazing how God worked it all out, because there was room for all of us on a flight that would get us to our destination on time. All we needed was a ride to the airport, which was about a 45-minute drive away. The owner of the dealership then told one of the salesmen to take the owner's personal car and give us a ride.

We tried to pay him, but he would not take a dime for helping us with our trip. In fact, the owner told us to call and let them know when our return flight would arrive, and they would pick us up. As it happened, they brought our car to us at the airport when we returned so we would not have to make the trip back to their business to pick it up. That was so very nice of them, and we truly appreciated their kindness. In fact, years later, when we were driving through that area, we stopped and thanked them again!

During our tenure in Washington, Craig married his high school sweetheart, Melanie, and they had a beautiful wedding with George performing the ceremony.

Craig and Melanie in 2005

They decided to reside in the Washington area and when our first grandchild joined the family, they named her Celina Jo. She was a beautiful baby and the pride and joy of our family. I guess the first grandchild is always special, but then we feel the same way about each one as they join the family.

Over a year later, Amanda Jo was born. Craig and Melanie dropped Celina off at our house on the way to the hospital and they just arrived in the nick of time for the doctor to deliver the baby. It was a close call, and Craig was so relieved he did not have to face the challenge of bringing his second child into the world himself!

Since we were taking care of Celina, we decided to take her on a little trip. We went over to the Gettysburg area and visited a farm where they raise miniature horses. They were so small and so cute that Celina was not afraid of them. We had a great time there, and then made the trip home so she could get acquainted with her new little sister.

Meanwhile, after much prayer and hard work, things started looking up and God was blessing Soul's Harbor Lighthouse Church once again. It is so wonderful to know that God likes to work when nothing else will! Even though trials and tests come our way, and sometimes we make huge mistakes, God is ready to forgive when we repent. There are times when we do not know what decision to make or which way to turn, but God is always standing by, ready, willing and able to help us. He will lead us in the right direction if we will only pray and seek His guidance. What a wonderful, loving Heavenly Father we serve!

However, the discouragement that hit my husband when we returned home from India kept haunting him, and without fully understanding what was happening, he became totally depressed! Naturally, he had a hard time being a pastor, which made things very difficult. But, when he entered the pulpit to preach, the anointing of the Holy Spirit came down upon him and he ministered in a beautiful way. As soon as the service was over, though, that depression jumped back on him full force.

This lasted for quite a while, and feeling the only solution to the problem was to resign and leave the area, he did just that. First, he met with the church board and informed them of his decision. Then he announced it to the congregation. It was a very difficult time for everyone, but the end result was that the Soul's Harbor Lighthouse Church would be dissolved. There were bills to be paid, so we had to take care of them somehow. There are times when we just cannot understand what God is doing, but we have learned He does all things well! God was not through with us in Western Pennsylvania, but knew we needed time to be restored in body, soul and spirit, and had to leave for a while. Ministry was our life, so we decided to go back into the evangelistic field traveling from church to church as doors opened up to us.

There was one lady that was saved under our ministry that wanted to talk to us when she found out we were planning to travel again. She is a very sweet lady and an excellent cook. Gladys Weigand was sorry we were leaving, but told us we would come back. Of course, because of so much heartache and pain we suffered while being there, we did not think we would ever return.

She knew we would be gone for weeks at a time and volunteered to pick up our mail and forward it to us, no matter where we were at the time. It was so sweet of her to offer to help us in this way, and she was very faithful to take care of our mail for a long time. She also told us she had an extra bedroom, which she called a "prophet's chamber" and offered it to us anytime we were in the area. Gladys had three daughters, and years before when her husband passed away, she went to work to provide for her young children. She had worked hard all her life and is a wonderful Christian lady. I am proud we can call her our friend.

Her daughter, Carol, and her family would come down from New York to visit her, and her granddaughter, Wendy, thought our Scot was really cute. None of us knew at that time that she would one day be our daughter-in-law.

Chapter 44

Moving Times Three

We thought it would be best to leave the area and searched for a house down south and rented one in Cleveland, Tennessee. It was a lovely new house that suited our needs very well. We thought it was centrally located considering our evangelist ministry.

Scot traveled with us. He continued running the sound for our ministry, doing a very good job just like his brothers had done. Scot was still single at the time, that is, until he and Wendy decided to get married. The wedding would be in Bergen, New York, where Wendy lived with her family. So, we made plans to travel that long distance.

The wedding was lovely and George helped perform the ceremony along with the pastor of the church where Wendy and her family attended. Scot stopped traveling with us and they made a home together there in New York. He found employment and they rented an apartment. It was the next year that their first child was born. We were in South Carolina at the time, and quickly made arrangements to travel north to see our first grandson, Calvin Scot, Jr. He was so sweet, and it was a joy to be able to cuddle him in my arms. We had a nice visit, but our time was limited so we had to be on our way.

Scot and Wendy in 2008

Even though depression lingered with George, we continued to minister in different churches and the Holy Spirit was so faithful in each service. However, when the service was over, George felt life-less inside and wondered where God was! This was a very difficult trial for him, but God was faithful to see him through.

Eventually, the depression left and once again we were called to pastor a church in 1984. This time, it was in Anderson, Indiana.

It was always amazing to see how God would use circumstances to bring us to churches He wanted us to pastor. There were times when we did not even know the person that called us, but after arriving at the church soon became good friends. God blessed in our services and ministered to the congregation in a wonderful way.

Meanwhile, Scot and Wendy had moved back to Pennsylvania but wanted to move with us to our new location. Scot, Jr. was just a baby, but he made the trip just fine. Nevin also went with us, and we moved into a lovely three-bedroom ranch style home in a nice neighborhood, which was just perfect.

God blessed in our services and ministered to the congregation in a wonderful way. There was a family that attended the church and their teenage son had become an alcoholic. His parents wanted so desperately for him to accept Christ so his life would be changed. They knew if he continued to drink as he had been doing, that his life would soon be over. After much prayer, he answered the alter call and gave his heart and life to Jesus. There was such a dramatic change in him that people were amazed. He knew immediately he should quit drinking alcoholic beverages, and that he should leave his old friends behind and make new ones. He continued attending services and was growing spiritually, which thrilled everybody, especially his parents. God worked in other hearts and lives while we were there, and everything went well.

About a year later, when we accepted a church in Crisfield, Maryland, Scot and Wendy moved back to Pennsylvania. It was 1½ years later that our second grandson, Michael, was born, and

Timothy came along approximately 2½ years after that. Then, last but not least, Joshua arrived almost five years later. Each one was adorable, and all of them are very intellectual and talented in different ways. For example, Timothy was mechanically inclined and was also awarded a full scholarship; and Joshua, at the age of 12, generously gave time to tutor other students after the school day.

When we moved to Maryland in 1986, a young Christian man named Kent moved with us, because he wanted new surroundings. He and Nevin became like brothers and worked together in construction while we were there. He was also a blessing to the church. During the services, I played the piano, Kent the drums, and Nevin played his bass guitar, which provided music for the song service. It seemed to be enjoyed by all.

God provided a lovely ranch-style house for us to rent and right behind it was the backwaters of the Chesapeake Bay. There was a place where we could put crab traps if we wanted to catch live ones. We had never done that before, but it did look interesting.

While we were there, Nevin met Bev who later attended one of the services. They spent much time together and it wasn't but a few months until a wedding was being planned. Since we had plenty of room, we invited them to live with us and we all got along great together.

I recall one weekday when Bev and I went shopping together. We spent several hours at a mall and enjoyed the day and our time together. Surprisingly, at work the next day, when her co-workers asked what she had done on her day off, they seemed shocked to learn Bev spent the day with her mother-in-law on a shopping trip. I was truly pleased we could set such a positive example for good relationships between in-laws.

Crisfield was a small town where seafood was plentiful. Huge festivals were held there each summer and people came from all over the United States for the occasion. That small town became packed, and we wondered where everyone stayed while they were there because the town had very few motels.

Several miles south of Crisfield was a place called Smith Island. The only way you could visit there was by helicopter or by boat across the bay. One day, we received a telephone call from a gentleman on the island. He asked if we would come and hold a revival meeting there. They had scheduled Rev. Dan Betzer, but he was unable to fulfill his commitment. We were glad to oblige and had wonderful services that week. Our hostess made some of the best crab cakes we had ever eaten, and of course, the crabmeat was very fresh because they were catching them daily.

When we first arrived at the island, we felt like we had stepped back in time. The roads were very narrow, and there were only two or three cars anywhere to be seen. Most people rode a bicycle or walked, and it did not take very long to walk all around that small island. Nobody ever seemed to be in a hurry. There was an elementary school there, but when children reached high school age, they had to ride a boat over to Crisfield to attend high school. We enjoyed the time we spent on the island, as it was very peaceful and quiet, which was very refreshing.

We learned we would be grandparents again because Bev was expecting their first child. Things went very well at the church in Crisfield, and God blessed the services in a great way. We raised enough money to pay off the mortgage on the church building, which was a tremendous blessing. Then God spoke to our hearts in 1987 and let us know it was time to go back to Washington, Pennsylvania to finish our work there. He knew we were now restored and ready to fulfill His Will in that city.

We presented our resignation to the church board and to the congregation. Then we made a trip to Pennsylvania to locate a house we could rent. A friend of ours had one on Lakeview Drive that was available, so we rented it from him and made the move. We had moved so many times before that it did not take us very long to pack our belongings, load the trucks, and begin our journey. Of course, we did have help this time from Kent, Nevin and Bev, and they all moved with us. We unpacked and settled into our two-story country home, and then proceeded to find a suitable building where we could have regular church services.

We decided to look at the local Y.W.C.A. that had a nice large auditorium with a baby grand piano on the stage. There were also rooms that were available for Sunday School classes, so we signed a contract and began to hold worship services. God blessed in a wonderful way, with souls being saved, bodies healed and homes rearranged. The congregation grew quickly and many families were making our new Lighthouse Church their home church.

There was a comical incident that happened while we were living on Lakeview Drive that we will never forget. The weather had cooled down, and one evening we were sitting in the den relaxing when Nevin thought he would play a little trick on us.

He had several firecrackers and twisted the fuses together to make one big one. They were old, so he didn't know if they would even work, but laid them on the heat register in the kitchen anyway and lit the fuse. The explosion was much louder than he had anticipated, and it scared us half to death! We had some problems with the furnace, and this noise sounded like it had exploded. Then, when the furnace came on, it blew the tiny shreds of paper all over the kitchen. That joke turned out not to be as funny as Nevin thought it would be, but we can laugh now when Nevin relates the story to others.

Chapter 45

A Granddaughter Arrives

We made it through a frigid Pennsylvania winter. Spring finally arrived and temperatures climbed with gentle winds blowing. It always feels good to look outside and see new life all around us. The grass was turning green, and flowers were bursting through the soil reaching toward the sun.

Our new grandchild was not due until late April and Bev wanted some experience in caring for a baby. So, she took a temporary job as a babysitter for the lady that prepares our taxes. Susan and her husband, Melvin, had adopted an adorable baby boy. His name is Zachary and he was about six months old. She wanted a reliable sitter that would be available until April 15 when tax season would be over, and asked what would happen if Bev delivered her baby before that date. I knew how much Bev wanted that job, so I told Susan I would be available to help out should the baby arrive before the due date.

It was early Sunday morning on April 10, 1988 when we were awakened from our sleep to discover Bev was in labor. Nevin took her to the hospital and stayed with her while we prepared for our Sunday morning worship service. On our way to church, we stopped by the hospital to see how she was doing. George wanted to pray with her, so he took her by the hand and began to pray. Just at that moment, she had a contraction and squeezed his hand so hard that it hurt. He quickly ended his prayer and left the room, because he did not want to be there when the baby was born!

We drove to church and the worship service was wonderful. Everyone was thrilled to learn we would soon have another grandchild. When the service was over, we went back to the hospital to see Bev and she was still in labor. However, later that day we had a new granddaughter they named Lindsey. She was a beautiful baby with dark eyes and dark hair.

Our fellowship always schedules a Northeast Regional Conference in the month of April in Lancaster, Pennsylvania, and we had already sent in our reservations to attend. However, I was not going to be able to go because I had promised to baby-sit if Bev delivered early, and I definitely planned to keep my promise.

Our good friends, Henry and Betty Howells, were kind enough to stop by and give George a ride to the Conference. I really appreciated that, because I needed our car while he was away. So, for the next five days, I drove about 20 minutes each morning to pick up my little charge and brought him to our house, because I also needed to be there to help Bev, especially the first few days after she came home from the hospital.

After taking care of the needs of Bev and Lindsey and preparing meals for the day, I took Zachary back home so he could be there when his mother arrived home after work. I have always enjoyed taking care of babies, so it was a real joy to care for such a well-behaved child during those five days. Recently, I saw Zachary again and he had grown into a handsome young man, and was very mannerly and courteous. Of course, he had very good training from his loving parents.

Chapter 46

A Home Of Our Own

The day came when we needed to look for another house to rent and found one on the west end of town, which was very nice. It was in a small housing development and had a screened-in back porch, which we enjoyed immensely. It was while we lived there that God blessed us with the opportunity to have a house of our own.

A friend of ours called George one day, and asked him to take a ride with him. They drove out West Chestnut Street and then turned onto Old National Pike. They proceeded to the top of a hill and turned right into a driveway. There on approximately 2½ acres of land sat a farmhouse, which was about 125 years old and in need of much repair.

At one time, it had been a beautiful old homestead, but had not been properly cared for over time and stood empty for many years. He said he would put up the money if we would do the work to remodel the house. We could then either buy it or it could be sold. George looked at the foundation to see if it was solid and it looked good, so he thought the house was worth remodeling.

We had never had the privilege of owning a house, and the idea sounded wonderful because we had moved many times during our married life. So, George told him we would be very interested in doing the remodeling project. It took many months to get all the work done, and he worked extremely hard. I helped him when I could, and Nevin helped, too.

We had only worked a few weeks and had not yet replaced the doors or windows when someone broke into the house and stole some of our tools and other items. George had bought some of those tools from an elderly gentleman in Jersey Shore many years before and they could not be replaced. He was very disappointed, but there was nothing we could do about it; however, we made certain the doors and windows were replaced as soon as possible, and then we kept the house locked when we were not there.

Over the next two years, we worked on that house when there was extra time because the ministry came first. We actually built a house within the walls, because the house had double brick walls, but no insulation. We found out the bricks were made right there on the property. Therefore, there was a variation of colors in the bricks, mostly red shades. However, after all those years, the bricks were not pretty anymore so we had the house painted a beautiful cream color and trimmed in a lovely shade of blue. The porches had deteriorated long before this time, so they had to be replaced.

We had to install new wiring and plumbing, including telephone lines, and all the walls needed to be insulated. Once that was finished, the drywall could be installed. There was no bathroom on the first floor, and no laundry room at all, so we put an addition on the back corner of the house that included a hallway and those two rooms. It worked out very well, but drilling through that brick wall to make a doorway was probably the hardest and dirtiest job of all.

The house consisted of six large rooms, with three upstairs and three downstairs. When we laid out the plans for the kitchen, I asked George to build an island for me because the room was square and it would fill the center very nicely. He did so, and installed the sink and dishwasher there. We then put plenty of cabinets and counter space all around the room. He also built a beautiful light box above the island that brightens the room and enhances the soft hues of light yellow walls with green accents.

After about two years, the work was almost finished and George talked to the owner about the possibility of us moving into the house because it was very vulnerable sitting there all by itself with no other house in sight. After all that hard work, we certainly did not want someone to break into it and destroy the interior. He agreed we could move in, and then we would decide what to do with the house after all the work was completed.

After living in a ranch style house, and making the move to the farmhouse, we could not believe how much more room we had. In fact, we didn't even have enough furniture to fill the rooms. There was a huge dining room, but we had no dining room furniture, so we put our kitchen table and six chairs in it. The only thing we had left to put in the kitchen was a card table with four chairs, but we were happy to be there.

We have a huge lawn, and when grass started to grow, we pulled out our power mower. It took us many hours to cut two acres of grass, and even when Nevin helped us with his power mower, it still took us most of a week to finish the job. Of course, by that time we had to start all over again. We definitely needed a riding mower, so we scouted the area to find a good used one, and with God's help, found one we could afford. We were so grateful, because we could finish cutting the grass within three hours. That truly was a blessing from God!

When Old Man Winter made his appearance once again, snow began to fall one day and was still coming down when we awoke the next morning. When the last flake had fallen, we went out to see how deep the snow was. This storm dumped nearly 30 inches on western Pennsylvania. It was beautiful to behold from our hilltop view, and looked like a white blanket was covering everything in sight. It was so clean and pretty.

We have a very long driveway, so in order to leave the house, we would have to shovel our way out. George and I donned heavy coats, hats and gloves, put on our boots, and picked up two shovels and began to dig. When you are not used to shoveling snow, it can tire you out rather quickly. We had to take breaks every little bit, but we finally made two pathways to the street. At least, we could get our car out if we needed to go somewhere.

Scot called us and during our conversation, we told him we had shoveled our driveway and he immediately said, "Dad, you shouldn't be shoveling that much snow. You could have a heart attack. Please don't do that again!" So, eventually we bought a snow thrower, and that was a wonderful investment!

When the time came to discuss the possibility of our buying the house, we found out the asking price would be out of our range. Therefore, the house was put on the market for sale. Needless to say, we were disappointed but were allowed to stay there until a buyer came along.

Almost five years later, we were still living in that house, and no one showed interest in purchasing it. Our sweet friend, Gladys, was praying that the house would be ours, and she believed God for the answer. Her prayers reached God's throne, because He caused us to meet a couple that became very dear to us.

We met Donald and Betty back in 1983 when we were invited to minister in a church in Maryland. The services were very rewarding and God blessed many hearts in a special way. Donald and Betty invited us to stay in their home and were very kind and gracious hosts. Their infant son was named after his dad and just as cute as a button!

Our acquaintance with them blossomed into a family style relationship. Over the years we enjoyed watching their son, Don, grow into a handsome young man, and we especially take pleasure in him calling us grandpa and grandma.

When Donald and Betty found out we had never owned a house and had moved many times over the years, they told us they would like to help us buy this house because they did not want us to ever have to move again unless it was our decision to do so. We will truly hold this special couple very dear to our hearts.

George went to talk to the owner, and told him we would like to buy the house and had a couple that would help us. The many hours we had worked was taken into consideration and deducted from the asking price. He gave us a good deal, and we rejoiced and thanked God that we finally had a house we could call *"our home."* What a wonderful blessing!

There was an open garage near the house, and even though we would have enjoyed parking the car in it, we had no place to put George's workshop. He has all kinds of power tools, and enjoys making beautiful cabinets, knick-knack shelves and furniture. So, our only option was to close-in the garage. He spends many hours there working and making beautiful wooden treasures. The items he makes are difficult to find in stores, because he uses solid wood. Most factory-made furniture has a veneer finish.

There were a lot of trees at the edge of our property, and some had died and fallen to the ground. George had put a wood burning stove in his workshop, so during summer time, he worked to make sure he would have firewood for the winter months. He talked to the owner of the property next door, and he was happy for George to clear the fallen trees and use them for firewood.

One day, Nevin and Lindsey stopped by for a visit when George was out cutting wood. After talking to him, Lindsey came into the house with me. It was not long until Nevin rushed in, took me aside, and explained his dad had been using the chain saw and as he cut through a log, he brought the saw down too quickly and cut a big gash just above his knee. He would definitely need stitches. Nevin was going to take him to the hospital, and said I should stay home with Lindsey because he did not want her to know about the injury until it had been treated. Thank God, a few stitches closed the gash and he would be fine in a few days.

Chapter 47

God's Healing Hand

George and I had always been rather healthy and were grateful to the Lord for that. However, intermittent severe pain over a few months made it difficult for George to stand, but God helped him finish the sermon one particular Sunday morning. He finally made an appointment with the doctor and learned he had a hernia and needed surgery. This was a real test for him, because we had no insurance and no savings to draw from, and we were just living week by week with the small salary the church could provide.

One of our friends encouraged us to inquire about funding assistance to see if we were eligible, but George really did not want to do that or take funding allocated to help others. However, the pain got so intense that he had to do something, and that was our only alternative. As we sat in that office waiting for his name to be called, we looked around the room at all those unfortunate people and learned what it felt like to have to ask for financial help. God was showing him what others had to go through, and gave him empathy for the less fortunate.

When we finally talked with an agent, he examined our financial records and told us that because of our low income, the entire cost of the surgery would be covered. When we left there, I felt elated, but George felt defeated. He had prayed for many people to be healed of physical problems, and God had performed some incredible miracles! Now, he prayed for his own healing, but it had not come and he could not comprehend God's plan.

The surgery was scheduled, and all went well. He was an outpatient, so he was allowed to return home that afternoon. However, he was in a lot of pain and it was difficult to stand. Our bedrooms are upstairs, so he planned to sleep on the couch in the living room.

There was a widow lady, Anna, who had no children and came by our house quite often to take us out to eat. When she found out he was not allowed to walk up steps for a few days, she immediately ordered a hospital bed to be brought to our house and set up in our den. We deeply appreciated her kindness, and it truly was a blessing to us.

A week or so later, our friend, Pastor Domer Snyder, had a guest speaker at his church in Blainesburg, Pennsylvania, and we had the opportunity to attend. We arrived a few minutes early, greeted our friends, and sat down. Domer asked if we would sing a special number for them that evening, and we were happy to do so. We sang, "What A Healing Jesus," and when we were finished, Domer related to the congregation that a young girl named Heather who attended their church had a blockage in her urinary tract and was scheduled for surgery the next day.

Normally, the guest speaker would be asked to pray, but Domer felt he should ask George to pray. At this point in time, George was still wondering if he would ever pray for the sick again, but he could not tell Domer that he would not, so he knelt down in front of the young girl and prayed a simple prayer asking God to heal her.

The next morning, we were busy around the house when the telephone rang. It was Domer, and he told us Heather's parents took her to the hospital that morning for the surgery. They checked one more time to make sure the blockage was still there — *but it was gone*. They were praising God for healing her! God had used this incident to let George know that He had everything under control, and to keep praying for the sick, because He still heals! We do not understand why everyone is not healed, but it is not our place to question God.

Chapter 48

Serving God and Helping Others

It was sometime later that the furnace at the Y.W.C.A. quit working properly. We held our services in the gymnasium and there were three sets of double doors on the outside wall. One Sunday, we noticed it was snowing and the wind started to blow really hard. When snow started coming in through the cracks at the doors, it did not even melt, so you know how cold it was in there. So, we had to look for another place to hold our services.

There was an old hotel in town, but it had been turned into small apartments and quite a few elderly folks lived there. There were several meeting rooms available, plus a ballroom in case we needed a larger room. We rented the Vernon room first, and it had a small piano in it, so at least we had some accompaniment for our singing.

Some of the folks who lived there started coming to our services. We welcomed them with open arms and they were very pleased. There were two in particular that came on a regular basis. A gentleman by the name of Harold, and a lady named Helen. She was a sweet lady and one day asked us to come up to her apartment for a visit. While we were there, she told us her husband died several years before and she lived there all alone, but she had made friends in the building and enjoyed their company.

She also told us that she and her husband owned a cottage over near Phillipsburg, Pennsylvania, and they had enjoyed going there with their family. The children grew up and went their separate ways, and then her husband died and she had not been over to see the cottage for years. We offered to take her there to see if everything was alright, and invited Harold to go along. The trip was very nice, and since it took about 3½ hours to drive there, we stopped and had a nice lunch together.

Everything was fine at the cottage, so we returned home. Then one day, Helen called and told us she thought she would sell the cottage because the children did not go there anymore, and there was no need for her to keep it. However, there were some items in the cottage she wanted and had no way of getting them. Since we had the van, we volunteered to go get them for her. We told our sons where we were going, and also mentioned we would try to make it back home the same day. However, if the trip took longer than planned, we might stay overnight somewhere on the way home. We did not want them to be concerned about us.

After arriving at the cottage and loading the van, we headed for home. When we neared Altoona, it was time for dinner, so we stopped to eat and then continued on our journey. We were traveling on a four-lane highway and had traveled several miles when George noticed our headlights were getting dim. Then we heard what sounded like a small explosion, and he saw a flame shoot out from under the van. He immediately pulled over to the side of the road and turned the motor off, but when he tried to start it again, it wouldn't start.

Since it was getting dark, George did not want to leave me alone in the van while he went for help. We thought for sure that someone would stop to lend us a helping hand, but that ended up being just wishful thinking. One car going in the opposite direction crossed over and pulled up a short distance behind us. When George opened to door to ask them to make a telephone call for us, they drove away.

Normally, we take some snacks and drinks with us on a trip, but for some reason we did not take anything this time. So, we were grateful we did have a chance to eat dinner. We waited for hours and no one stopped. It was early evening, so we looked out the window and watched a train slowly make its way around the hillside. We finally decided to try to sleep a little bit, which is very difficult to do in a work van. The seats did not recline and they are not very comfortable for sleeping.

The night air grew cold, and we were not dressed for the cooler temperatures. However, we did thank God that Helen had asked us to bring some blankets back for her, so I found them among the stuff and we were able to cover up and keep warm.

It seemed like night would never end and it was just about dawn when George told me we should start walking for help. It was also starting to sprinkle rain, and I wondered if we should go at that moment. However, it must have been a leading from the Lord, because we had no more than stepped out of the van and started to walk, when a trucker pulled over to the side of the road, and the driver asked if we wanted a ride. We could not thank him enough, but he told us he could not let us walk up that mountain, because it was quite a few miles before we would find a service station.

He dropped us off, and we called AAA, and had the van towed to a repair shop. George had been talking about purchasing a cell phone, but until that day, I not seen the need for it. Today, we both have cell phones, which have been a very useful tool.

Chapter 49

Down The Wrong Pathway

C raig and Melanie had attended The Lighthouse Church and it was a joy to see them sitting in the services week after week. One day, though, things changed in their lives and they would soon learn the road ahead was going to be a rocky one. Craig worked for Ryan Homes, and was the best truck loader they had. So, when his supervisor was transferred to Georgia, he gave Craig, among others, an opportunity to transfer with him.

Craig moved first to look for a place for his family to live. Melanie and their daughters, Celina and Amanda, joined him a little later. Craig had always been a hard worker and earned his pay; however, he was by no means rich. Therefore, when an opportunity came along to earn big bucks, it was a temptation he could not resist.

Of course, what he was getting himself into was disastrous! A so-called friend told him he could make thousands of dollars each week if he would just sell illegal drugs. He started out by selling just a small amount, and was enticed to sell more with the lure of easy money and plenty of it.

One day, he flew to the state of Oregon to purchase some drugs, and how he brought them back on an airplane without being detected is still a mystery to us! Unknown to him and those living in the house, the police had them under surveillance and it was a good thing he came home when he did because his life could have been in jeopardy.

One weekend Craig sat down on the bed and counted out thousands of dollars, which was income from drug sales. He rented the house he was living in, but was building a new one. He had seven Harley-Davidson motorcycles, which he thoroughly enjoyed riding with several of his biker friends. They would hire a sitter for the girls and take off with their friends on weekends.

One day, he received a telephone call from one of his friends and was asked to bring some drugs to Pigeon Forge, Tennessee. The friend was staying in a motel and asked Craig to meet him there. Another friend who lived in the area had invited Craig to come for a visit so they could do some target practicing. So, Craig stored his guns in his saddlebags, and took some drugs with him and Melanie. Another couple also went along, and it was a blessing in disguise that the girls did not make the trip that time.

When they arrived at the motel, they went to the room and met their friend. They were only in the room for a minute or two, and he was taking the drugs from his pocket, when the door to the adjoining room burst open and the local police rushed into the room. They looked at Craig and asked if he was Bonz (pronounced bones—his nickname at the time), and he said yes. They threw him down on the bed and handcuffed him as well as the others, and took all of them to jail. Craig had enough money with him to post bail for two of them, and quickly acquired funds for the other two to be released so they could all return home.

They were told to make a return trip to Pigeon Forge the next weekend to see the bondsman. So the next Saturday, they made the trip again and found a parking place right in front of the building. Celina and Amanda were with them on this trip and they all got out of the car. They did not know it, but federal agents were waiting for them, and immediately jumped out of their vehicles. When they asked if he was Craig Van Riper, and he said, "Yes, I am," they grabbed him.

This time, there were federal charges that included selling drugs. They had to stay in jail over the weekend because they could not post bail until Monday. The bondsman was kind enough to take the girls home with him, and his wife cared for them until Monday morning when Melanie was released. I am sure it was a very difficult time for all of them, especially for the girls having to stay with people they had never met.

Melanie was allowed out on parole, but they would not release Craig. It would be several years before he would again be free. They took him to Chattanooga, Tennessee and held him there in jail until a hearing could be scheduled.

Back when we still lived on Lakeview Drive and were remodeling the house on Old National Pike was when we received the telephone call from our son Nevin, who was living at home with us at the time. He told us we should come home because he needed to tell us something very important.

When the probation officer told Melanie they were going to inform her parents, she begged him not to call. However, he did call, and her mother, apparently skeptical about the call, hung up on him. After recovering from the shock, Shirley Craig (Melanie's mother), then called our house. At the time, we had no idea what was going on, or what Nevin had to tell us that he did not want to say on the telephone. When we arrived at the house, we realized why he felt he should tell us face to face.

Nevin told us the whole sad story and it seemed unbelievable. How could our son, who was reared in a Christian home, become involved with selling drugs? After they moved to Georgia, though, they no longer attended church services and became involved with drugs and drinking. Satan saw an open door and worked overtime to send them down the wrong pathway.

Chapter 50

Our Hardest Day To Face

The next morning and with broken hearts, we loaded our luggage in the car and made our way to Chattanooga. We were deeply troubled over what had happened, and selling drugs was something we totally disapproved of. But, he was our son and we loved him dearly, so we wanted to be there for him. We didn't know what we could do to help, but we knew we needed to make this trip.

It was not easy to talk during that long drive, because the very painful thought of our son being in prison caused tears to flow. Therefore, most of the time our car was engulfed in silence as both of us were lost in our own thoughts concerning the uncertainty of what the future would hold for our son.

When we finally arrived at the jail and walked through the doors, a deep feeling of sadness overwhelmed us. We had been in jails before, but it was always to ministers to others, never to visit one of our own family. What would we do, and what would we say? We were told to sit down and wait, so we sat on a bench in the hallway.

It seemed like hours had passed, and then we saw a young couple walking toward us. They were smiling and talking about something wonderful, so I looked up and said, "It sounds like you have some good news." They were extremely excited as they told us how they had just led a young man to the Lord. They often came to the jail to visit inmates and to tell them how much Jesus loved them and that He wanted to come into their lives. That was wonderful to hear, so we told them who we were and they introduced themselves as Steve and Denise Truxell. We began to tell them about Craig, and did not know what his reaction would be, but asked if they could possibly visit him when they made their next trip back to the prison. They assured us they would, if he approved their visit. They went on their way, and we sat patiently waiting to see Craig.

Finally, we were told we could see our son and they led us back through the prison to the area where he was being held. We could not even hug him because we were separated by glass. It was like a bad dream, and I thought that at any minute I would wake up and realize none of this had happened. However, that was not the case and the road in our future would be very rocky before becoming smooth again.

Thank God, Steve and Denise were invited to visit with Craig, and they became friends. After a few visits, they began to ask him about his life and he told them he came from a Christian family and had accepted Christ as his Savior when he was young. However, he had rebelled and went the way of the world. They told him how much God loved him and wanted him to come back to the cross, which would change his way of life. That day, Craig realized he had drifted far from God and that the Holy Spirit was drawing him back, so he asked Jesus to forgive him and rededicated his life to God.

We returned home with heavy hearts, because we knew Craig was facing a prison sentence. We were faithful to attend the regular church services; however, it was very difficult to join in the singing. For many weeks, George could hardly preach because the tears would not stop flowing. Some members of our congregation were very sympathetic and prayed with us that God would intervene and work everything out for our good and His glory. We were so grateful for them, because we needed their support so desperately.

There were others that left the church, believing we had not properly reared our sons. That was so hard to understand, and even caused us more heartache and pain. So, we just had to lean heavily upon our Savior and take one day at a time as He slowly healed our broken hearts. He was the Rock we could stand on, and He brought us through that trial, which was the hardest one we had ever faced!

We have learned that when children reach the age of accountability, we can no longer make their choices for them. We can teach them the right way to go, but if they rebel and take the wrong paths, they will have to give an account to God for their actions. Some sins have much greater consequences than others, and we do reap what we sow, Christians and non-Christians alike.

Chapter 51

Facing The Judge

Melanie hired an attorney and his fee was astronomical, but to our dismay he did not even show up for a bond hearing. Therefore, Craig was held at the Chattanooga prison until the day he would face the judge. Naturally, we made the long trip once again to be with our son, not knowing what the outcome would be.

As we sat on a bench in that courthouse, we looked up and saw Craig coming down that long corridor with a marshal on each side of him. Craig was a tall man with a long stride, but he was handcuffed and shackled and made his way by shuffling his feet. I jumped up and ran toward him, wanting to give him a big hug, but the marshal said, "Sorry ma'am, but you can't touch him." I cannot begin to describe the pain I felt inside as I turned and slowly made my way back to my seat, trying to hold back tears.

After they took him into the courtroom, we also went in and sat down. The judge sentenced Craig to eight years, and although Craig hoped Melanie would not be sent to prison, the judge sentenced her to five years. We were just grateful the sentence had not been more severe, because it could have been. Now, all of us would have to deal with the problems that lie ahead, and the future certainly looked bleak.

The judge gave Melanie time to go back to Athens, Georgia to settle their affairs and get everything in order before she had to report to Danbury, Connecticut to serve her time. After she packed all the boxes and was ready, Nevin went down to drive the truck to Pennsylvania for her. She stored their belongings, and began to make the necessary preparations for her impending confinement.

Her main concern was finding a home for their two daughters while she and Craig were away. Although we knew it would be very difficult to be grandparents with the responsibility of parents, we welcomed them into our home.

When it came time for Melanie to go to Connecticut, we told her we would drive her there. She was going to fly, but we just could not see her having to make that trip all alone. At least, we thought we could be of some moral support to her. We drove during the day and most of the night to get there on time, and made it with very little time to spare. It was springtime and we actually ran into a snowstorm, but God gave us a safe trip, for which we were very grateful.

Melanie has allergies and must have medication to relieve reactions that could be life threatening; however, there were delays in getting medication to her. Distressed over the delays, she telephoned her mother and explained that her throat was so swollen, she felt like she was going to choke to death. Shirley called the allergist who then called the prison and worked out a quick resolution.

Chapter 52

A Family Reunites

After Craig was sentenced, they placed him in Tallahassee, Florida, and we took the girls down to see him. Our first visit went as well as could be expected, but we could only make that long trip a couple times a year. Then we found out we could request that he be moved closer to home so we could visit him more often. After being transferred to several different places, they finally moved him to Morgantown, West Virginia, which was less than an hour away and we could take the girls to visit him each week. We could not call him, but they did allow him to call us if he reversed the charges. So, he called home quite often to talk to the girls, because he missed them so very much.

Meanwhile, Melanie became very upset because she blamed Craig for her imprisonment. She had told him over and over that they were going to get caught selling drugs. Of course, he thought he would never get caught; therefore, he would not listen. She later told Craig during a personal visit that she no longer wanted to stay married to him and did not love him anymore. He was stunned and crushed, but could do nothing while incarcerated.

It was quite a challenge taking care of Celina and Mandy. Our finances were rather limited at that time, because of the new church we had founded. However, God took care of us just like He always had in the past. Bills somehow got paid and there was always food on the table. We may not have had everything we wanted, but we certainly had everything we needed, and that is what God has promised His children.

Week after week, we would take the girls and make the trip to the prison in Morgantown. We would sit at tables and visit during the allotted time. We were glad to see Craig, but it was difficult to leave him there when it was time to go home.

God did intervene for Melanie, and she was granted an immediate release after 3½ years, and flew home to be reunited with her daughters and family. She rented a trailer and moved into it with the girls. She did not start attending church services right away, but when invited she did attend an annual Lighthouse Church banquet. She came with her sister, Lori, and our son Scot and his wife, Wendy. Melanie always loved music, so she enjoyed the concert we had after dinner. As she sat there, the Spirit of God spoke to her heart and impressed upon her to dwell on the good part of her marriage to Craig, and, if she truly wanted to be happy, she must forgive Craig and stay with him. Right then, she allowed God to totally change her attitude toward her husband. That truly was a miracle!

The next time Craig called home, Melanie answered, and he asked to talk with the girls but they were not home. So, she took that opportunity to tell him that God had changed her feelings toward him and that she still loved him and would wait for him. Craig was elated because he still loved her and wanted to spend the rest of his life with her.

Chapter 53

Free At Last

It seemed like an eternity, but finally the years passed by and the day arrived when Craig would be released. We could feel the excitement in the air, and could hardly wait to see him.

It was an awesome feeling for Craig to know he was finally *FREE* after 6½ years, which had seemed like a lifetime! He felt badly he had missed those years with Melanie and his daughters. Now, he would begin to make up for those lost years! Thank God, his confinement time had been shortened because of good behavior!

The first meal he wanted back home was an old family southern favorite, "chicken and dumplings." And, I was happy to make it for him and the rest of the family. What a homecoming! We had such a great time, because finally the whole family was together once again.

Craig and his family immediately became a part of The Lighthouse Church family, and I will never forget the first service they attended. It was a beautiful time together, and the Holy Spirit was very prevalent in that auditorium.

It brought back to mind a Promise God had given to us years before that I had held onto and kept in my heart all those years. When we were traveling in evangelist ministry, we had stopped in Washington, Pennsylvania one day to pick up our mail. Gladys held it for us, because we let her know we would be traveling through the area. I noticed there were several letters from our bank, and that puzzled me. When I opened them, they were stating that our account was overdrawn, so we were facing finance charges we had not counted on. I always made sure the bank statement balanced with my figures, and I knew I had not written checks for money that was not in the account.

It was Saturday, so there was no way to contact the bank to see what had happened. We needed to travel south for our next engagement, and late Sunday afternoon we decided to stop near Richwood, Kentucky to spend the night. I told George I must take out the checkbook and try to find my error. He went out to ask the motel clerk if there was a good church nearby that we could attend that evening. He was back in a matter of minutes and said I should get ready to go because it was almost time for the service to start. I mentioned I had to find out what the problem was with our bank account, so maybe I should stay and work on it. He told me if I put it away for a while, maybe it would be easier to find later on, so we got ready and went to church.

It was a huge church, and the auditorium was almost filled to capacity. We did find a seat and enjoyed the service very much. The people were very friendly and the pastor presented an excellent sermon. When the service was over, we walked back to the door to leave and the pastor stood there shaking hands and speaking to everyone. When he shook hands with us, he asked if we would step aside and wait a few minutes because he wanted to talk with us.

It was not long until he joined us and asked who we were and where we were from, so we told him we were from Pennsylvania and were traveling evangelists. He talked with us for a while and then prayed with us, and then told us that God had given him a word for us, and this statement was what I held onto for many years: "When your sons return, it will be like a new beginning."

How would he know that we had sons, unless God told him, because we had not mentioned our family at all to him in our conversation?

He also told us we would again have a pastorate, and that we would be loved like never before. We were thrilled with his words, and could hardly wait for God to fulfill that Promise! It took years for that prophecy to be fulfilled, but when Craig and Melanie walked through the church door that day, it truly was like a new beginning for us, and the church!

On returning to that motel room, I immediately began to search the checkbook for a possible mistake, but I could not find one. This was very perplexing, but I decided to put it away for the night, knowing I could call the bank the next day. When I talked to one of the tellers, she told me how sorry she was we had been charged for overdrafts in our account, but she had tried to reach us by telephone and could not get us because we were traveling.

While we traveled from state to state, we would send our deposits to the bank by mail. I would allow enough time for them to be deposited, and then write checks to cover our bills.

Together, we went over the account and discovered they had not received one of my envelopes, which had several deposits enclosed. We don't know why that envelope was lost in the mail, and to our knowledge, it was never found. We contacted the churches where we had ministered, and told them the check they had given to us had been lost in the mail. All of them, except for one, sent us a replacement check, and we were so thankful for their kindness. However, we still had to pay the bank charges, which amounted to a large sum. But, we were grateful the problem was solved, and we could continue on our journey.

Craig and Melanie then became a vital part of our ministry, because Melanie has a beautiful singing voice, and sang with her sisters throughout the years. She sang solos and also began to sing with us again in a trio. Craig became our sound engineer and did a wonderful job. In fact, over the years all three of our sons learned how to run the sound system for us when we sang. It truly was a blessing to have Craig and Melanie home again!

Chapter 54

The Terrible Flood

The year was 1993. We were watching the news on television and saw the heavy rains and terrible flooding in the Midwest. We were especially interested in Quincy, Illinois, because that had been our home a few years before. We heard people from Quincy, Massachusetts were planning to go help victims of the flood in their sister state. At that moment, God spoke to George and asked him what *he* was going to do to help those people.

Since we had no extra finances, he thought we should share this need with our radio audience on The Beam of Hope Broadcast in Pittsburgh, Pennsylvania. We thought we would give our listeners an opportunity to help the victims, and were thrilled with their response.

With starting a new church, George had been doing some carpentry work to supplement our income and had a work van, which we could use to transport items to Illinois. We learned the things needed most were cleaning supplies and paper products. People started responding immediately and as items were delivered to our home, our porch became filled with boxes.

News teams came from television stations in Pittsburgh and they ran the story that night during their evening news broadcast. One crew came to the church and another to our home to film loading of the van.

George and Nevin left the next day to deliver the goods to people in Quincy who needed them so desperately. Through that news report, a lot of other people learned how they could help with this project and we soon had enough items for a second vanload.

Those people were so appreciative of the help that had come their way from folks in western Pennsylvania. Many of them had lost so much, and it would take years for their lives to get back to normal. Some had lost their homes and everything they owned, and they were desperate.

While George was there, he learned about a family that had lost their home, and the Lord laid it upon his heart to help them. When he spoke with them, George discovered the man of the house, Dale, had been a teenager when he attended the church where George had been pastor in Quincy. It was amazing to us that the Lord aided in that connection, and they were thrilled when George told them he would try to raise some money to help build a new house for them.

The family could borrow a portion of the money needed but not enough, so when George came home, he mentioned on the radio broadcast that he would like to build a house for this family. He wanted nothing for himself, but money was needed to buy materials. He also asked if there were any others willing to donate their time to help him, which he would surely appreciate.

It was wonderful the way folks responded. Five other men offered to go with George and help for a week, and they did a tremendous amount of work during that time. After a week or two of rest, George traveled back there for about two more weeks of working many long hours. If memory serves me, about $11,000 came in through our radio audience, and that bought a good bit of materials back then.

George would be gone for a week or two at a time and spent many hours working on the house. Of course, he always took Sunday as a rest day. He later decided he could get more work done if he flew out instead of driving.

Since I was babysitting Lindsey while Nevin and Bev worked and it had been a while since I had gone to North Carolina to visit my mother, I took this opportunity to go.

So, Lindsey and I traveled to Beckley, West Virginia and stopped to see Basil and LaVaughn, and spent the night there. It was a nice break in the trip, and we left early the next morning to arrive in Waxhaw that afternoon, which is located just south of Charlotte.

We spent several days with my mother, also with Pop and Dolores, who lived nearby. We had a wonderful time together, and then left on Friday so we could be home for the weekend.

We again stopped to spend the night in Beckley, and left early Saturday morning. We had only traveled about 30 minutes when Lindsey asked, "Grandma, what is that smell?"

I looked in the rear view mirror and saw smoke billowing into the air. I immediately pulled to the side of the road and told her I had no idea what was wrong with the car. We had just passed a car dealership, so I told Lindsey we would walk back there to see if we could get some help.

As I was helping her out of the car, a young man who was driving the other direction stopped to see if he could give us a ride. That was so nice of him, because we were on a four-lane highway and it could have been dangerous for us to walk very far. After he dropped us off, we went inside and they told us their mechanic was not on duty that day and there was no one that could help us.

The only thing I could do was call my brother. There was no answer at the house, so I called his office. He had his own insurance company, and his daughter, Melody, answered the phone. Basil was not there, but she would locate him and he would come as soon as possible. It was not long until he arrived, and he had brought another man with him. They raised the hood of the car and discovered a hose was leaking fluid.

They drove to a nearby town and could not purchase the hose, but did buy some clamps. It did not take them long to cut off the defective part of the hose, and clamp the remainder back in place. It seemed as good as new. Then, Lindsey and I drove on home without another incident. I thanked the Lord we were not far from Beckley when that hose broke and He kept us safe along that busy highway!

When December rolled around, a lot of people in Quincy were still struggling, and we wanted to help them enjoy the holiday season. So, we raised enough money to buy everything needed for a complete Christmas dinner for 25 families. George was already in Illinois and I wanted to go help him with the Christmas baskets. Lindsey also wanted to help, so Nevin drove us out to Columbus, Ohio, and we flew from there to Quincy.

We went to the store together to buy all the groceries for the gift baskets, and the church where we had pastored years before allowed us use of their large foyer to put the orders together for each family. The families then came to pick them up and were so thrilled that people who did not even know them, cared enough to help. Of course, we could have never helped them if the wonderful people in western Pennsylvania had not donated the money in the first place.

After Dale's house was under roof, the family could borrow enough money to get the inside finished, so George did not have to go back anymore. They were so grateful for all the work that was done and for the beautiful house they could now enjoy. One weekend, they came out to see us and meet our congregation because some of them had helped, too. We had a great get-together and are planning one day to make a trip to Quincy to see them and their beautiful home.

Chapter 55

Our Own Church Building

As more people came to the services, we realized we needed a P.A. System in order for everyone to hear what was being said. We had one we used when we traveled, so we brought it to the hotel and used it each week. Of course, that meant it had to be set up before each service, and taken down afterward. It took a good bit of time every Sunday to do that, so we began to look around for a building of our own.

We looked at many buildings and vacant land, but found asking prices to be out of our range. It became discouraging and then one day George decided if we were to have a church building of our own, God would have to send someone across our pathway to tell us about it. We had done all we could do, so the rest was up to God, and in His usual way, He responded rather quickly.

George went to the post office to pick up our mail one day, and there was a letter from the superintendent of the Wesleyan Methodist

Churches of Western Pennsylvania, and he mentioned he heard we were looking for a church. He lived in Dubois, which is about a 2½ hour drive from us. Now, how in the world did he know that? We are not sure, but to make a long story short, they had a church they wanted to sell, and it was just about one block from our home. We made the trip to his office to discuss the matter, and were thrilled when we left.

All the details were worked out, we raised some of the money, and the bank loaned us the rest to purchase it. We were so thrilled to see how God worked when we could not do a thing! What a blessing it was to be able to have church services whenever we wanted to, and leave the P.A. System set up all the time.

We were also traveling to Pittsburgh each Saturday for our radio broadcast, but after a while, decided it would be so much more convenient and cost-effective to be able to broadcast from our new church building. We mentioned the need to our congregation and to our radio audience, and within a short time had enough money to buy the necessary equipment for our own radio studio. God is so good!

George is pictured in the radio studio minutes before
going on the air in The Lighthouse Church on a Sunday morning
prior to the regular church service.

Chapter 56

Mother Moves In And Moves On

My mother was living with Dolores and Pop in North Carolina, but decided she would like to come to Pennsylvania to visit with us. She also wanted to visit my brother, Junior, and his wife Rhoda, in the central part of the state. While she was here, she told us of her plans to move into a personal care home, but I didn't think she really wanted to do that. So, George and I talked it over, and asked if she wanted to come live with us for a while. She was glad we had asked her, and did move in with us.

Things were going pretty well, and then one day we had an emergency call and had to leave for a while. Nevin had stopped by the house while we were gone, so he stayed with mother until we came back home. He then took me aside and told me mother seemed to be disoriented and didn't know why she was here. We knew she had early stages of dementia, and maybe that was the problem. From then on, we could not leave her alone. I am so grateful for dear friends like Boots (her nickname), Gladys, and Melanie, who came to stay with mother at one time or another while we were busy with the ministry. Also, for Craig and Melanie, who came to stay with her when we attended our International Conference in Florida.

One day, I was working downstairs when she called to me from her bedroom. I went up to check on her and realized she had a dizzy spell, had fallen and could not get up on her own. To this day, I am amazed that I could pick her up and put her on the bed; however, I understand that when an emergency arises, an adrenalin rush allows us to do things we normally cannot do.

She was with us for almost a year, and as church attendance grew, so did my responsibilities. I did all the office work and helped with other facets of our church ministry, including visitation. Plus, I had my own housework to do as well as caring for my mother, so the load became too heavy. George could see I was being affected physically and emotionally, and realized that somehow, things had to change. Mother constantly talked about going back to the central part of the state and thought she would really enjoy living there again. So, George and I discussed our options.

Finally, George told me he knew I would not want to make such a decision, so he decided we would have to put mother in a personal care home. So, we took her back where she wanted to be, and trusted she would be content there. We visited her quite often and she was doing well, and was always happy to see us.

On December 11, 1997, I was working at my desk in the church office when I received a telephone call from the lady in charge of the care home. She told me mother had been taken to the hospital but had no further report at that time. She did explain mother and her roommate were preparing to go to breakfast, but her roommate was not quite ready. Mother was resting on the bed when the roommate was ready shortly after, but mother did not respond when she called to her. She ended the phone call saying she would call back as soon as she received word on mother's condition.

It was not very long until she called back and said mother had passed away. An aneurysm near her heart ruptured, so she died quickly and woke up in heaven! She did not suffer, so that gave us some consolation. Scot happened to stop by the church office that day just after I received that call, and we shared that heartrending moment together.

We sadly made all the arrangements and traveled to Mifflinburg for the viewing and funeral. Mother had written down her desires for the funeral service, so we tried our best to fulfill her wishes. Her former pastor from North Carolina came to officiate at the service, and did a wonderful job.

Basil and LaVaughn came up from West Virginia, but he was not well at the time. He had suffered a heart attack and then cancer invaded his body. He was taking chemotherapy treatments, but was able to schedule them so he could attend the funeral.

My niece, Teresa, relayed this beautiful story to me later, which Rhoda had described to her shortly after mother's passing.

Mother was fortunate to get to visit with all her children during the week before she passed away. They had all stopped in with their spouses to visit at one time or another.

She had a wonderful visit the evening before her passing when Basil and LaVaughn and Junior and Rhoda spent time with her in her room along with another couple, long-time friends Charlie and Jenny Harris. Pop calls Charlie "a real guitar-pickin' man!" Mother had sung and played her banjo and fiddle in their musical group for a while. All shared an exceptionally joyful visit playing their instruments and singing, something Mother enjoyed immensely.

During the evening, Rhoda noticed Mother was just bubbling over with great happiness and grinning from ear to ear. Believing it to be more than just the joy of playing their instruments and singing, Rhoda felt compelled to ask, "Why are you so *happy*?" Mother, wearing the most glorious smile, replied with excitement, "I'm going to heaven!" And she did, the next morning.

It was only a few months later that my father-in-law passed away, so we traveled to Milton for his viewing and service. My sister-in-law, Louise, was the church pianist, so I offered to play in her stead so she could be with her family.

With our parents gone, we began to realize we were now the patriarchs in our family, and that was an awesome feeling. You just don't think about things like that when you are younger.

We made occasional trips to Beckley, West Virginia to visit Basil because the doctor had given him only six months to live.

He was able to stay in his home for a while, but eventually had to be taken to the hospital. LaVaughn was always by his side, taking care of his every need. He surpassed the predicted time, and lived for two years.

One day, we received a telephone call informing us of Basil's demise. With saddened hearts, we made the trip to Beckley. LaVaughn asked if we would sing, "What a Healing Jesus," so we were happy to oblige. Their pastor officiated at the funeral service, and I will always remember one statement he made, which was, "A Prince has fallen." That was so true, because Basil was a wonderful brother, father, husband, and Bible teacher.

It is hard to believe we lost three of our loved ones within a year, but with them knowing the Lord as their Savior, they will be in heaven waiting for us to make our entrance. Then we will have a wonderful reunion!

Chapter 57

Trips To The ER

It was early one Sunday morning in 1998 when George woke me up and told me I should take him to the hospital because he was in terrible pain. I dressed quickly and we left. We drove through town and when we came to a red light, he told me to keep driving, because at 2:30 a.m., there was no traffic. I did slow up to make sure no car was coming, and then proceeded through the red light. I was only a block away from that first red light when we heard the siren from a police car. I pulled over and George told me to get out of the car and tell the officer what was wrong.

When I opened the door and started to get out, the policeman called out to me, "Lady, you know, I am supposed to pull my gun if you get out of that car." I immediately responded with, "Sir, I must get my husband to the hospital." He believed it to be an emergency and instructed me to follow him. He led us to the emergency entrance, where I stopped, and he took George inside while I parked the car. The policeman put him in a wheelchair, and because George had his hands on his chest, the attendant thought he was having a heart attack.

Since it was the wee hours of the morning, I really did not want to call anyone, but I knew our sons would want to know. Naturally, they were all in bed asleep, but it did not take them long to arrive at the hospital. We sat in the waiting room and waited and waited and waited. It seemed like forever before they allowed us to see George.

The doctor would not give him any medication until they found out what was wrong. Meanwhile, he was telling them he could not take the pain much longer. After tests and x-rays, they discovered he was having a gall bladder attack, and they were able to get the pain under control.

It was soon time for our church service to begin, so I rushed home to change and arrived at the church in time to play the piano for the song service. Our Associate Pastor, Don Amon, filled the pulpit that day. Our congregation was sorry to hear about their pastor and they prayed that God would touch him.

George eliminated fatty foods from his diet to avoid another painful gall bladder attack. His main diet was fruits and vegetables and the pounds melted away. Two weeks later, he had surgery to remove his gall bladder.

Medical science had come a long way, so microscopic surgery was an option, which required only a few small incisions. Therefore, recovery time was much less than it would have been in previous years. The surgeon told George that after surgery, he could eat anything he wanted and it should not bother him. Well, George must have been the exception, because some foods still bother him to this day.

Several years later on a cold wintry day, I had just washed my hair and was going to blow it dry when I heard George calling to me from downstairs, and his voice sounded urgent! I rushed down to the kitchen to find him wrapping a paper towel around his thumb. He had been working in his shop cutting some boards on the table saw, when he accidentally brought his left hand too close to the blade. I did not know how bad the cut was, and he didn't show me, but said I should take him to the Emergency Room immediately.

With a wet head and wearing sweats, I grabbed a jacket and the car keys, and off we went! I never leave the house without making sure that I am properly dressed and my hair styled; however, this was an emergency and I had no choice!

I dropped him off at the entrance, and proceeded to park the car. Before I went inside, I quickly called Nevin and asked him to call Craig and Scot. Naturally, I broke down and cried when I started to tell him, and he thought I said his dad had cut off his thumb! Our sons and their wives, all rushed to the hospital to be with us, and we waited together until he was treated.

In actuality, the saw blade had ripped out a piece of his thumb, and it was unlikely that such a small piece could be stitched back into place successfully. It also had made a small cut in his nail. The doctor recommended that he see a hand surgeon in Pittsburgh. George thought he would need skin grafting and was very concerned about it. When the surgeon told him he would not be doing any skin grafting because it would not stay in place, George was so relieved that he almost hugged him.

He did have some therapy, and they bathed his hand in a special solution quite a few times. We changed the bandage often and in a few weeks were amazed at how the skin was starting to grow back together. It took about six months for his thumb to be completely covered with new skin; however, a lot of nerve endings were severed and part of it is still numb, and part tender to the touch. But, we are thankful he still has a thumb on that hand!

As a mother, I feel honored to have such a close family and privileged that they respond so quickly during family emergencies. Another memory that comes to mind is when my daughter-in-law Wendy took it upon herself to speak to hospital personnel and was able to get me into the ER for an update on George's condition.

Chapter 58

Our Beloved Family Pets

Throughout the years as our sons were growing up, they shared much pleasure in the family pets we were able to have in different houses as we moved around the states.

The most unusual pet was a duck Nevin had for awhile. It followed him around everywhere, and he had a great time raising it.

Most of our pets were housedogs, such as a poodle, terrier, and cocker spaniel. But, it seemed like we were never able to keep one very long because the time would come when we moved again, and they couldn't go with us.

However, when we finally settled down, we decided we needed a dog in our lives once again. Their excellent hearing also gives us a sense of security and warning when someone arrives at our home. We scouted the area and found a cute little mixed breed puppy that was part husky and part black Labrador retriever. We named her Princess and enjoyed watching her grow up. When she had her first litter, we were elated. She had nine puppies, but one was stillborn. She was an excellent mother and kept those little puppies clean and well fed. Her husky background resulted in two of the puppies having blue eyes.

It wasn't long until George had to build a small pen for them so they wouldn't wander out into the road. Once they were weaned from their mother, George fed them regular dog food. They looked so adorable as they welcomed him with their little tails wagging. They then scrambled all over each other trying to get to the food. When they had devoured every bite, Princess would clean them until they looked like little balls of black and white fur.

As we look back on those days, we realize it was pure pleasure watching that canine family grow up. It wasn't long until we could let them out of the pen to run all around our big yard. They had such a time!

I recall one day when our granddaughter played with them in the yard with her long hair braided into one thick braid down her back. As she romped with them on the ground, one little puppy latched onto her braid with its mouth and hung on. It was quite an amusing scene as they played in the grass.

All too soon, they were grown and needed a home with another family, because we certainly didn't need nine dogs. However, George did want to keep one, so we were privileged to rear one that had blue eyes. He was so loveable and we named him Duke. He and Princess had great times together, and if she barked, he barked. It was almost funny, but he was mimicking his mother, and that was good.

One thing they did that surprised us occurred every time they heard a siren or fire whistle blow. Both of them would curl their tails, throw their head back and howl. It was totally different than anything we had ever seen before, but kind of nice at the same time.

It was a sad day when Princess developed cancer and had to be put down. Duke missed his mother so very much.

George had wanted a German shepherd for quite a while, and when the opportunity came our way in the year 2000, we drove out into the country and brought home a beautiful puppy.

George was thrilled and Champ became a wonderful friend and fantastic watchdog. No one enters our yard without his warning bark, and we can tell the difference as to whether it is a family member or stranger. He also lets us know if someone walks on the road in front of our house. He has become a wonderful companion and excellent guard dog.

Chapter 59

Serving Others In A Time Of National Crisis

It was on Monday morning, September 11, 2001, when the telephone rang as I was working in my office at The Lighthouse Church when the caller, a young man who attended our services, had some devastating news.

Gary told me an airplane had just crashed into one of the twin towers in New York City. The United States of America was under attack. Minutes later, another airplane flew into the second tower! People were rushing down corridors and stairways trying to leave the buildings; however, there were many that could not reach the point of safety. Their lives were lost in a matter of minutes, and many homes were filled with grief and sorrow because those loved ones would never return home.

Very shortly after that, we received news that an airplane had crashed into a field near Shanksville, Pennsylvania and there were no survivors. If it had remained in the air a few minutes longer, it could have struck an elementary school filled for a typical school day. Many parents were thanking God that day for protecting their loved ones.

A few minutes later, we learned another airplane crashed into the Pentagon! The enemies of America certainly were trying to eliminate our citizens. Our granddaughter, Celina, was working out of Washington D.C. at the time, and living in Frederick, Maryland. She had gone to her car, but had forgotten something and as she returned to the house, heard the telephone ringing. It was her dad, Craig, telling her not to go to work that day because America was under attack.

During that week I talked with our friend Cindy in Greensburg, and she told me of the need for volunteers to help The Salvation Army at the Mobile Canteen. It was manned onsite many hours every day to provide food and drinks for the clean-up crew at the crash site. We told her we would be happy to lend a hand.

The next day, we drove the two hours to the site and arrived in the afternoon. We parked our car in a field with other vehicles, and rode in the back of a jeep to the Canteen to relieve other workers who had been serving for several hours. The Canteen was about 1,000 yards from the crash site and that was as close as any volunteers were permitted, but we really couldn't see very much from that distance.

There were numerous workers, such as FBI (Federal Bureau of Investigation) agents and Rescue and Recovery personnel from NTSB (National Transportation Safety Board) who were doing their jobs and trying their best to locate information concerning the accident. It had to be a very complex task for them, and as they came for a bite to eat, we could see the sadness in their eyes because they could find very little of anything to give to the remaining loved ones. We did learn later on that an open Bible was found near the wreckage, which was a miracle because the heat had been so intense that almost everything was burned.

Our shift was scheduled from 2 to 6 p.m. but we were there until 11 o'clock that night. Finally, someone came to relieve us, but we had no way to get back to our car. It was very dark and we could not see our hands in front of us, so we couldn't walk. That was when I saw two young men wearily walking up from the site, and they stopped by the Canteen before heading out for the night. I became very bold at that moment and asked, "Could we please get a ride with you because our car is parked down in a field?" They were very cordial, and as we rode along we learned they were FBI agents.

We returned the next week to help again. This time, our friend MarJean Miller went with us and we worked together for several hours. We felt it was our privilege to be able to do something to help, even if it was just to serve food and beverages.

It just so happened that we were at the Command Center when the buses came by that were filled with loved ones and families of the deceased. They were coming to view the crash site. How difficult it must have been for them because they had not only lost loved ones, but could not have a customary funeral service for them.

Everyone lined the road and all policemen stood at attention. The remainder of the crowd waved as the buses slowly made their way past us. It was the same day First Lady Mrs. Laura Bush came to pay her respects and console the broken-hearted and grief stricken family members. They were so honored that she took the time to come and deeply appreciated her kind words and loving concern during their time of sorrow.

Chapter 60

Recordings

George and I started singing together before we were married in 1955, and a few years into our marriage considered making a recording. Our first project was back in the 1960s when we recorded our first two singing recordings in a Pittsburgh, Pennsylvania studio. Then when we were ready to make our third recording, we drove to Harrisburg, Pennsylvania. We decided to go to Nashville, Tennessee for the rest and were so glad we did because the talent there is just amazing! I would sit down at the piano and play our song one time for the musicians, and they wrote down numbers while I played that corresponded to notes and chords to help them depending on the instrument each played. When I stopped, they started playing the song, just as though they had known it for years.

Over the next 25 years, God allowed us to make eleven recordings of our singing. Most were recorded in Nashville but the last one was recorded in Bill Gaither's Studio in Indiana. Nevin harmonized on some of our later recordings.

A local mall held concerts several times a year and we were invited to sing there during half-hour segments throughout the day. Scot was about 5 or 6 years old when making his debut and people enjoyed hearing him sing. Eventually, they began setting up chairs to accommodate the crowd but no matter how many chairs they set up, there always seemed to be people standing.

When Scot was ten years old, he traveled with us to Nashville. We were making a new recording and he recorded two songs of his own on a small 45 rpm record. He did a great job! Many years later, when we pulled some of our old songs out of the archives to put on CDs, we added Scot's songs. They were entitled "Mama Always Had A Song To Sing" and "Which Road Leads To Heaven." On the latter one, George and I sing the verse and Scot sings the chorus. So, his songs are also heard in hundreds of homes.

Years later, our daughter-in-law Melanie sang with us as a trio in local churches and in all-day concerts. We also made a professional cassette tape recording together in Nashville. Many thought she was our daughter, likely because of her blonde hair color being similar to mine. Melanie and her sister, Lori, and I made a cassette tape recording as The Lighthouse Trio. A few years later, Melanie also made her own solo recording called "Whatever It Takes" with the lyrics of the title song being her own.

In 2001, I recorded my first instrumental recording, playing the piano and dubbing over it with organ and strings. We sold so many

CDs and cassette tapes that I was amazed. So, the following year, I recorded another one. It was also well received, and I just could not believe how many people love instrumental music. Two years later, I made my third and last recording. This time, Nevin played bass guitar, which added a wonderful dimension to the recording.

It was a pleasant surprise when the telephone rang one day and a lady told me how wonderful it was to hear my instrumental recording while she was having an MRI at the hospital. She said the piano music was very calming and soothing while she had to remain perfectly still for quite a while. There were several different recordings to select from, but she wanted gospel music and chose mine. It is a blessing to know that my music can calm the nerves of individuals who have to endure such tests.

My niece, Teresa, is a beautiful lady and talented in many ways, and especially in writing and photography. She also encouraged me to record instrumentals, so, when I completed my projects, the cover pictures were all produced by her artistic touch. She was a tremendous help to me, and I truly appreciate the many times she went out of her way to be there for me. We are alike in many ways, and enjoy spending time together. Even now as I relate these stories, she is helping me with the preparation of getting this book in print and designing its cover.

Chapter 61

Traveling Across God's Country

During our years in evangelistic ministry, we made two trips to the west coast. Seeing the natural world that God has created can be breathtaking. Each state has its own distinctive beauty with awesome views, and its own uniqueness, like deserts that seem to go on forever to mountains in the distance.

I will never forget how surprised I was when we saw the Rio Grande River. Expecting extraordinary magnificence, we were quite disappointed to discover what looked more like a creek than a river. And, it was very shallow, which was also a surprise!

The Petrified Forest was amazing, and Mount Rushmore was a sight to behold. Then while driving through the desert, we turned onto a road that led to an Indian Village where we found their museum to be very interesting.

As we traveled along one day, we found ourselves near Yellowstone National Park. Because the sun was disappearing rather quickly, we decided to stop for the night and found a cottage just outside the park. That evening, the owner asked if we would like to go see some moose, and we were thrilled he invited us. They were enormous, standing about six feet tall just to the shoulders. God truly has an imagination that shows up in his creations, which are magnificent!

The next day, we drove into the park and there was so much to see! Our only disappointment was that our time was limited to one day in the area. We did get to see Old Faithful, which was totally amazing as it spews forth right on time, every time. We also saw some other springs, but the day went quickly and we had to be on our way. However, we were grateful to be able to see some more of God's beautiful creations. How could anyone say there is no God?!

Day after day, as we drove mile after mile, the scenery became more beautiful — if that were possible. We saw fields of impressive wildflowers and snow-capped mountains in the distance. What a contrast that was, and yet we knew God had created all things well.

We ministered in several states, and then proceeded to Idaho and traveled along the Snake River for miles. It was beautiful scenery, but towns were few and far between. There were also very few restaurants, so when we finally saw a small diner, we stopped. It looked like a hunting cabin with a rustic interior and the food was delicious. It was there that we met a man and a woman we will never forget.

As we sat at a table, a couple walked in and I overheard him say, "Oh, I want some of their sausage and gravy on biscuits." Without thinking, I looked up at him and said, "They don't have any more." We had ordered the same thing, only to find out the couple at another table had taken the last orders. We introduced ourselves and learned George and Shirley Creighton were from Spokane, Washington. They had driven to the Snake River to do some white water rafting. Better them than us, I thought!

We invited them to sit with us and enjoyed the social time together after our long hours on the road. In sharing conversation, we noticed there was something different about them, which I reasoned later, was why I felt at ease speaking to them when they entered the restaurant. They were born-again Christians, and when they inquired about us, we explained we were evangelists from Pennsylvania. They wanted to know where we would be ministering, which was the following Sunday at a church with a congregation made up of mostly Native Americans but with a Caucasian pastor.

After inquiring about where we would be staying, which is usually in a pastor's home, they generously offered their cottage on Lake Coeur-d'Alene to us and said we were welcome to stay there. As it turned out, we were able to do so and stayed there for the weekend while we ministered at church. Their cottage was beautiful with three stories built right on the hillside by the lake.

George and Shirley surprised us when they attended the Sunday morning worship service and it was so nice to see them again. I am sure the service was quite different from what everyone was accustomed to, because all sat perfectly still and showed no emotion the whole time. However, after the service was over, they all gath-

293

ered around and commented how much they enjoyed it. So, I guess you cannot always tell what people are **thinking** by their facial expression!

Before George and Shirley left, they asked where we would be going next. We told them we had just received word that our next services had been cancelled and we were not sure what our plans would be for the next week. They immediately asked if we would like to stay in their cottage. No salary for a week is hard enough to deal with, but having to stay in a motel and eat in restaurants for seven days would certainly have been disastrous to our budget! Once again, God was looking out for us and met our needs!

Their cottage had a lovely deck, and since it was the slow season, it was very quiet and relaxing. We truly enjoyed the time we spent there, and invited them to eat dinner with us one evening. We had a great time together. He owned a grocery store, so they could not visit very often. Our immediate friendship seemed as if we had known each other for years.

It was amazing they would trust us, total strangers to them, to stay in their cottage, because it was completely furnished and included a wonderful stereo system with many recordings we could enjoy! But, that is what the "family of God" is all about! It is remarkable how God sends the right people along at the right time. We have kept in touch with the Creightons all these years, and they with us. They wanted to come out for a visit several times, but each time, they learned that another grandchild was on the way, so naturally that was their first priority!

Chapter 62

An Earthquake

California is a beautiful state. The weather was mild during our stay in July. Days were warm and pleasant, but evenings and early mornings cool enough to require a jacket. Actually, I think you could say it is almost the perfect climate. We were in Anaheim to attend our Annual Conference.

We were enjoying our stay very much, until about 2:20 one morning when we were awakened by a loud noise. The huge window in the hotel room was vibrating, and the hanging lamp over the table was swaying back and forth. We could hear water in the bathroom sloshing all around, and there were people out in the corridors, talking loudly and obviously frightened. We had never experienced anything like this before, so we called down to the front desk to ask what was happening.

They told us there had been an earthquake in Palm Springs, which was about 100 miles away, and we were feeling the aftershock. We were on the eleventh floor, so there was no walking outside. When George asked what I was going to do, I told him I was going back to sleep. There was nothing I could do about the situation anyway. After a while, things settled down, and I guess everyone went back to bed. We let our boys know we survived the earthquake!

I recall one young lady at the conference who was visiting California for the first time. Cindy loved it so much that she told her mother she would like to move there. However, after the earthquake, she changed her mind immediately. She was quite anxious to get back to her home in Alabama.

Chapter 63

Fishing For Salmon

A few years later, we were planning to attend our Fellowship Conference in Eugene, Oregon, so George called our good friend, Pastor Ralph Trask and asked him if it would be possible to hire a boat and plan a salmon fishing trip while we were there. Ralph said he would be happy to work out the details.

All the arrangements were made and there were about 12 men that went fishing that day on a ship named El Shaddai, which translates in Hebrew to mean God Almighty. The boats had not been out for several days because of stormy weather, and they probably should not have gone out that day because the waters were still very choppy.

George could not even sit in a swing without getting dizzy, so when the boat went out to the point where it dropped anchor, it began to rock back and forth. It was not long until he became very sick and began to throw up, which he hates to do. Someone told him to find something stationary to look at, which should help, but he could not see anything except for the waves.

When the first salmon was on his line, he was so sick he could not even reel it in. He told Pastor Denny Helton that he could have it, so Denny reeled it in and it was a huge one. After it landed in the boat, George was not prepared for what happened next. One of the crew members grabbed a piece of pipe and hit that salmon on the head to kill it, and he must have hit it too hard, because it's eyes popped out, and blood squirted everywhere. If George had not already been sick, that would have surely made him ill. He threw up several more times and also had the dry heaves. The waters must have been extraordinarily choppy, because most of the other men became sick, too!

When the boat finally docked, the men could hardly walk up the steps. One man went straight to the rail and threw up again! Several of us were on the bridge watching, and when George saw me, he yelled out, *"Call the paramedics!"* Another man quickly said, *"Don't say that, or someone will call them."* George immediately replie*d, "I want them to make that call, because I am sick."* But, we were unable to hear what was being said, so we did not make that call.

That evening, several of us went out for dinner together and as we were talking about their fishing adventure, George laughed out loud and found out very quickly that he was extremely sore from the dry heaves!

Ralph invited us to come to his church in Salem, Oregon to minister to his congregation on Sunday. We told him we would be pleased to come. We drove there on Saturday, and had a beautiful church service on Sunday morning. Afterward, we all went out to a restaurant for lunch. As we sat there waiting for our food, George began to feel ill again. He had to go outside for some fresh air, and after several minutes, began to feel better. It took him several days to recuperate from his salmon fishing experience, and to this day, I cannot get him to go on a cruise. He is concerned he would get very sick again, so he refuses to take that chance.

After ministering in several churches in the west, we headed back home and crossed the mountains in Montana. The scenery gave way to beautiful vistas and we enjoyed the ride. But, as we climbed one mountain, there was snow on the ground and the air turned very cold. Then, to our distress, a popping sound from under the hood was followed by steam rolling upward from our 1982 Oldsmobile. Naturally, we pulled to the side of the road to find out what was wrong.

We discovered a hose blew a hole and we were losing water. We had some snacks with us in the car and happened to have some celery and carrots in a container covered with water. So, we taped the hose, and then used a clean handkerchief to strain the water and poured it into the radiator. This helped us reach the mountaintop. There was a rest stop there, and we hoped to get more water. However, when we arrived, it was closed and by that time the engine overheated again. We wondered what in the world we were going to do! George referred to the area as no-man's land and regretted having no tools along. We coasted down the mountain and when we reached the bottom, there was a stream near the road. Does God provide, or what?!

Thank God, I had taken my boots with us. So, I offered to walk to the stream to get some water. George did not want me to go, but I certainly did not want him to go, because he had no boots in the car. Because of the snow, it was very difficult to get close enough to the stream, without sliding down the bank. Therefore, we used drastic measures and melted some snow and put it into the radiator. Sometimes, you just have to make do with what is available!

There were very few towns on that mountain road, and we did not know how far we would have to travel to find a service station and mechanic who could help us. However, it was not long until there was an exit sign, and we saw a very small town. We knew we had to have the hose replaced, so we pulled into the only service station in sight.

The mechanic looked under the hood and saw the hose that needed to be replaced. He told us he did not have the correct size, so he would have to travel about 30 minutes down the road to get the part. There was a small café nearby, so we decided to go get a bite to eat while we waited.

About an hour and a half later, he came back, but to our dismay, had the wrong part and had to go back again. So another hour and a half went by and finally he returned. It seemed to be such a hassle, but we found out that it was God's way of protecting our car and our lives! While he was installing the new hose, he spotted two loose bolts that held the alternator in place. One of them was ready to fall off, and that could have caused the alternator to fly into the motor, which would have been devastating. Once again, we thanked God for his blessings and goodness! He had allowed us to have a small problem with our car, to save us from an enormous one! George said, "Where God guides, He will provide."

Chapter 64

Building A House

There are times when an evangelist has no meetings, and that means no money coming in each week. So, when our friends, Don and Jean Arnold learned George is an excellent and skilled carpenter who could build houses, they asked if we would be interested in building one for them. They were in no hurry for it to be completed, so we could work on it when we had free time. It sounded like a good plan to us, so we agreed. The house was to be built near her parent's home. Plans were selected, and after some minor adjustments, we made preparations to begin construction. The finished structure would be about 4,000 square feet, so it would take a while for us to complete the job.

On our first trip to Cowpens, South Carolina, we met Jean's parents, Thad and Ethel Guest. We became friends almost instantly. They were such sweet people, and we soon found out what a great cook she was because she invited us to dinner. Homemade pinto beans, spiced cornmeal cakes, and fried potatoes had never tasted so good! There is nothing like good southern country home cooking!

Jean told us her Dad did not make new friends right away, so she surely was surprised when we told her he offered his pick-up truck to us should we need some supplies that were not delivered.

After the foundation was finished and blocks laid, we began to nail down the flooring. We put insulation underneath, and the work went well. Then one day as we were working, George stepped backwards and landed on the insulation instead of the flooring and fell between the floor joists. He scraped his side and did not realize it at the time, but also hit his elbow pretty hard. Later on, when he was driving the car, he reached up to adjust the rear view mirror, and I saw a huge lump about the size of an egg on his elbow. I exclaimed, *"Oh honey, your elbow,"* which startled him, because he had no idea it was so swollen. Even though we used cold compresses, it still took several days for the swelling to go down, but it did not slow us down with our work on the house.

George custom built all the cabinets in the house including the doors, and there were over 100 of them. He constructed them from black walnut wood, and they truly were beautiful. Years later, they still look perfect.

During the summer months, it can get hot and humid in South Carolina, so we would take a break in the afternoon. We would ride the short distance to sit under the trees and visit with Thad. We did not have to talk a lot, but just sitting there together was company enough. Ethel was still employed, so she was gone during the day but we would see her in the evenings. While we were there, they treated us just like family, and we appreciated that so very much.

They had a dog named Beau, and it did not take long for us to become friends. He would come up the little hill to the house and look around as though he was checking to see if we were alright. He would go back and forth between the two houses, and it seemed as though he was protecting all of us. Ethel told us that when we would have to leave for a couple weeks, Beau really missed us. And, when we were coming back, he knew it was us before they could even see the car. He would get all excited and come out to greet us.

One Sunday morning, we stopped by their house for a few minutes on our way to church, and they asked if we had seen Beau, but we hadn't. He had not come home the night before so they didn't know where he could be. None of us saw him for a couple days, so we thought something must have happened to him. Then, one day we looked in the ditch by the side of the road near their house, and there he was. Someone had hit him with an automobile and the impact must have thrown him into the ditch where he succumbed to his injuries. We all missed him so very much after that, and it just was not the same there anymore.

While we were working, Pop and Dolores, who had moved to North Carolina, brought their recreational vehicle down for us to live in while we finished building the house. We had been paying to stay elsewhere, so that was a real blessing to us. They even came down and worked with us several times while we were there. We enjoyed living in the trailer, because I could cook our meals, which made it very nice. We prefer home cooked food anyway!

One night, we had a humorous incident in that trailer. There was a narrow hallway that led from the living room through the sleeping area to the bathroom. There were twin beds—one on each side of that hallway. A door to the bathroom opened up between those beds. There was a mirror on that door, and we usually kept the door closed; however, that night we forgot to close it. For some reason, George woke up in the middle of the night, rolled over and opened his eyes, and saw someone looking right back at him, and it wasn't me. He yelled, which woke me up, and then he discovered he had seen himself in the mirror. That was so funny! We still laugh when we think about that night!

Most of the time, it was just the two of us working day after day. The men and women in the area were totally surprised to see me working right alongside my husband. They were actually shocked when they saw me on the roof, helping to nail down shingles. They just could not believe that a lady would help do *"man's work."*

One day, I stood on the ground looking up at the roof where George was working. I was responding to a question he had asked when I turned to look down, and what I saw on the ground scared me half to death! Not five feet away from me was one of the largest black snakes I had ever seen in my life. That was quite a shock to me, but he was probably scared too, and believe me, it did not take me long to put some distance between us!

There were trees and bushes nearby, and quite often we would stop and sit under the trees when it was time to eat our lunch. One morning, my legs started to itch, and I was totally surprised to see what looked like a rash on them. I had scratched them during the night without even realizing it. They were turning red and becoming very uncomfortable. Ethel suggested that I see the pharmacist at the drug store who could probably suggest a remedy. He believed I was having an allergic reaction to what looked like bites of some kind, so I bought some Hydrocortisone Cream, which helped alleviate the problem. However, it took several days for all the bites to disappear, and that was my introduction to chiggers.

One day, George was in the garage cutting wood for the front porch on his power saw, and when he had little pieces to be discarded, he threw them outside. Meanwhile, I would gather them up, and since they were of no value, I started a fire and burned them, which kept the grounds cleaned up. One time, I reached down to pick up a piece, and not knowing I was there, he threw another piece out the door. Out of the corner of my eye, I saw a shadow, and the next thing I knew, a small piece of wood with a sharp point grazed my check and hit my nose.

My first impulse was to cover my face with my hands. When he looked up and saw me, he realized what had happened and came running outside to see if I was alright. There was just a scratch on my cheek, which produced a small amount of blood, but it was not serious. However, I had no idea just how sore my nose was until I rubbed it the next day. But, after a few days, the redness and swelling left and I was fine again.

Once we had the house closed in, we decided to move inside where it would be more comfortable while we did the finish work. Again, Dolores and Pop came to our rescue and brought us a bed, chest of drawers, sheets and other necessary items we needed. What a blessing they were to us!

Nevin came down to stay with us for a while, and he worked on the house, too. He was a big help, because he had worked in construction for years. However, one day, as they were putting the flooring on the front porch, he stepped backwards and missed the floor joist. His foot hit the foundation and he twisted his ankle and broke his foot. It was not an ordinary break, so we had to take him to a specialist. Naturally, he left that medical center with a cast on his ankle and foot, which had to stay there for several weeks. That hindered him from working for a while, but there were some things he could do.

Craig came for a few days to help us with the work and later on, Scot came for a few days. So, it ended up being a "family affair," and we really appreciated all the help because that was a huge house and quite an undertaking for us. However, it was the way God provided for our needs when we had no scheduled engagements.

In the mornings, George liked to walk during his prayer time, and when the temperature was warm enough, he would go outside and walk on the front porch. Ethel was still working, so there were times when he would see her leave for work before dawn, and Thad always turned the outside light off when she left.

One morning, it was too cold to be outside, so he prayed inside the house. He glanced out the window and saw the porch light was on at Thad and Ethel's house, and he thought that was strange because it stayed on for quite a while. He decided to go to their house just in case something was wrong.

When he arrived, he saw a vulture sitting in the yard, which was very strange. When he went inside, he felt terrible, because Ethel told him that Thad had fallen in the bathroom and she could not pick him up. She had gone outside to yell for help, but we did not hear her. It was such a terrible feeling to know she needed us and we had no idea what was happening. A few days later, Thad was laid to rest and we all missed him so very much.

Since we could not work on the house on a regular basis, it took about two years for us to finish it. However, the day finally came when the last coat of paint was applied to the walls, and the last coat of varnish to the cabinets, and the work was completed. The house was beautiful, and the owners were thrilled with the work that had been done. We had spent so much time with Thad and Ethel that we felt like family. Even though we left the area, we still keep in touch with Ethel, and we consider her to be a wonderful friend.

Chapter 65

Blessings In The Ministry

During a broadcast one day back in 2004, I answered a telephone call and a lady named Kathy told me her husband, Kerry, was in the hospital in serious condition. She also said he was a faithful listener of The Beam of Hope radio broadcast. Her concern was that he had never accepted Christ as his Savior, and should he die, would not get into heaven. We prayed for Kerry that day and after the broadcast, I told George I strongly felt we should go visit Kerry. We needed to talk to him about his soul, and where he would spend eternity.

Right after lunch, we drove to the hospital and found his room. When we walked in and spoke to him, he immediately said, "I know who you are because I recognize your voice from the radio broadcast!" He was a large man with a striking long white beard and hair.

We had a nice visit with him, and then asked if he would like to accept Jesus Christ as his personal Savior. He told us he would appreciate it if George would lead him in the sinner's prayer. God gave him a tenderhearted spirit that day and his life was changed forever. And he knew it. He was sent home from the hospital, and for weeks to come, he and Kathy drove to The Lighthouse to attend our church services. They told us how happy they were to be welcomed into our church family.

A few months later, Kerry went "home" and Kathy asked if we would have the funeral service. We felt it a privilege to do so. We were so glad we listened to the leading of the Lord and visited him in the hospital that day. That is one of the many blessings of being in the ministry.

Relating the story about Kerry has reminded me of another soul being saved when he was watching our weekly television program on WTAJ-TV Channel 10 in Altoona. He was an elderly gentleman who lived with his daughter in Everett, Pennsylvania. She wrote to The Beam of Hope Telecast and in her letter made the following comments concerning his salvation.

She and her father attended church together on Sunday mornings, but she was concerned about his salvation. She said in her letter that she would always remember one Sunday morning when he had already dressed and was waiting for her to finish dressing so they could leave for church. He settled down in his recliner in the living room and turned on the television to pass the time. Just as she was coming out of the bedroom, there on the screen was Pastor

George Van Riper telling his audience that without being "born-again" we cannot enter the gates of heaven. Then he mentioned that he would lead anyone in the "sinner's prayer" that would like to do so. As Pastor Van Riper prayed, she was extremely touched to see her father raise his hand and hear him pray that prayer, too. She was so thrilled and thanked God for dealing with his heart at that time, because within 24 hours he left this life, and Praise God, entered the gates of heaven!

Chapter 66

The Bat Dance

Brace yourself for another hilarious story, this time about a camping vacation! George and the boys planned a trip for some fishing and other recreation. But, this story is best told by our son, Nevin, so here is his recollection of events.

In the summer of 2004, my dad, brothers and I decided to take a few days to go fishing and just spend some time getting to know each other again. My brothers and I were in our forties and over the years, due to raising families, moving, and other life issues were not as close as we once had been. This seemed like a great time to renew our family ties. Years before, as a family, we had taken a vacation at Cook Forest. So we decided to make another trip there and rented a log cabin.

Shortly before our departure date, my youngest brother, Scot, received news that his oldest son would be deployed to Iraq.

Unsure of the exact day his son would leave, Scot decided he should stay home.

Early one Monday morning, Dad, Craig and I, said our good-byes and jumped in Craig's leisure van and headed out. The four-hour trip went by quickly and before we knew it, we were parked in the driveway of a beautiful cabin nestled in among the tall pines. The peace and quiet were overwhelming.

The cabin was roomy and very rustic. A small galley kitchen was surrounded by a living room with a fireplace, an eating area and bath. Two bedrooms were downstairs, and a loft with two more beds overlooking the living area finished off this true log cabin. Dad and Craig took the two bedrooms and I claimed the loft. Our first night there, Craig made the observation it was so dark when you turned the lights out, you couldn't tell if your eyes were open or closed.

The next morning, the canopy of pines made it hard to tell if it was cloudy or the sun was shining. A stone fire pit greeted you as you walked out the back door and although there was another cabin within eyesight, the seclusion was wonderful. We spent the next few days fishing the Clarion River and its tributaries and enjoying our drives as we looked for wildlife. Our visits to the gift and specialty shops were fun, and our adventure on the miniature golf course left us in stitches, we laughed so hard.

One of the highlights of our trip was a visit to the whitetail deer farm. Living in southwestern Pennsylvania most of our lives, white-tails were a common sight, but the deer on this farm were extraordinary. Their body size was impressive as well as their antlers.

Standard whitetails, white deer, albinos and a mix of the standard and white deer made quite a scene. A museum of Pennsylvania wildlife rounded out the experience. As impressive as all this was, the thing that left the biggest impression was the glass case in the entrance to the deer farm that held two live timber rattlesnakes. Big, ugly, and mean were the three adjectives that first crossed my mind! I would not want to meet one of those in the woods!

After a full day, we settled in for our last night in the cabin. Falling asleep easily, I was awakened sometime after midnight by some shuffling or rustling noise downstairs. As I picked my head up off my pillow, I noticed a light was on downstairs and heard the strange noise again. Easing down the extremely steep stairs from the loft, the sight I beheld is forever etched in my mind. There stood my dad in his pajamas, broom in hand, swinging wildly. At first, I wasn't sure at what. My first thought was maybe he was sleepwalking (or sleep-swinging)!

Realizing I was there, dad informed me he had been awakened by a bat flying around his room and was trying to rid his room of the invader. I reasoned it might be a good thing to help dad out, but with no second broom available and the small size of the room I maintained my position outside the bedroom and watched the comedy routine unfolding.

In dad's younger years, he played softball and had been a fairly good hitter with a good swing. I figured, with dad's ability, this would be over quickly. What I didn't know was that dad was scared the bat would land in his hair! So, every time he would swing, he would jump back, which would throw his swing off and he would miss. The scene looked like this: Dad would take aim, swing and jump back simultaneously, thus missing the bat, and end with an exclamation of, "Dear Josephine" (Who she is, I don't know!) or "Oh my lands!" or "Oh man!"

During one such attempt, dad's resolve became more determined. His aim was focused, his swing very intense (this made his jump backwards more severe), and the result was dad slamming his hinder parts into the doorknob. "Oh, Dear Lord!" he yelled, grabbing for the injured body part. The problem now was that letting go of the broom gave the bat free reign of the room, so within a split second dad had rearmed himself and now his mission was resolute. The injury must have honed dad's skills because within a few seconds the bat was rendered unconscious and taken outdoors.

Upon returning, my dad "dropped trou" and pleaded, "Son, look at my butt, am I bleeding?"

"Whoa, whoa, whoa, dad," I exclaimed quite shocked, "this is closer than I planned on getting this week! Besides, you backed into a doorknob not a butcher knife. You are fine."

We returned to bed, and as I lay there trying to muffle my laughter, I hear dad thinking out loud. "Those things have fleas and parasites. I wonder if any got in my bed?"

"No dad," I replied, "I doubt if they had time to jump off while the bat was flying around your room!"

"Do you think there could be another one in here?" dad asks.

"I doubt that seriously," I answered.

During this whole episode, my brother Craig never got out of bed or said one word. At this point, he felt compelled to share some of his knowledge with us. "Well, I heard that bats mate for life," he chimed in.

"Really," dad said concerned.

"Thanks, Craig!" I replied.

Not hearing the flutter of wings, dad's imagination starts working. His mind took him back to the rattlers at the deer farm. Dad asks, "Do you hear that?"

"Hear what?"

"That noise. I think there are snakes in the walls." he answers.

"Dad," I attempted to assure him, "This is a log cabin. There is no *in the walls*. Can we go to sleep now?"

Sure that the danger was over, we all went back to sleep and the next morning headed home. My dad doing the "Bat Dance," is an image *I will never forget!*

Chapter 67

Loved Ones Serving In Wartime

When countries are at war, many families are faced with devastation, heartache and pain. It has been that way down through the centuries with the many wars this country has been involved with.

When our oldest grandson, Scot, Jr. was deployed overseas to Iraq in 2004, we were not sure what the outcome would be. Even though he was not on the front lines, he was still continually in harm's way with the sounds of firing artillery all around him. I cannot imagine the horrible feeling of hearing gunfire everywhere and wondering where the next bullet would land.

Our servicemen and women deserve much credit for the sacrifices they make in protecting our country and freedom.

In the spring of 2005, Scot, Jr. was allowed a short furlough, and it was so nice to have him home again. His mother, Wendy, was extremely happy because Scot had planned a party to celebrate her

40th birthday and Scot, Jr. was back in the states at that time. It was a wonderful time together as family. It was all too soon that Scot, Jr. returned overseas to serve several more months to finish out his year's tour of duty in Iraq.

We praise God that he was one of the fortunate ones who was able to come home after he served his time. We shall be eternally grateful to God for this blessing. However, our hearts go out to those who never saw their loved one again and had to grieve over their loss.

Chapter 68

Soul Mates Find Each Other

I believe Satan always works overtime to destroy God's children and he works especially hard on young married couples and families. Unfortunately, Nevin's marriage eventually ended in divorce. He was devastated and wondered why such a thing happened to them. He seemed to wander aimlessly for some time and prayed about it daily.

However, God is faithful to His children, and ultimately sent Jackie into Nevin's life. She seemed to be exactly what he needed. She later told us that Nevin is just what she needed, too.

Nevin and Jackie first met as teenagers in school, but had not seen each other for years. Both had some terrible disappointments in life and both had been divorced with children. Each was still healing inside from the pain and hurt when they met by chance one day in town.

They spent some time together and enjoyed each other's company. It didn't take long to get reacquainted and they fell in love along the way.

In 2006, they were united in marriage. Jackie has been a wonderful addition to our family, and we love her just like a daughter. We are truly pleased our oldest son has finally found his life partner and genuine happiness.

Nevin and Jackie lived near us in Washington for a while. Then a friend of Nevin's invited them to move to Florida and Nevin, an ordained minister himself, answered God's call to work as an associate pastor in a church in Orlando. They made the move and loved living down south. However, later on and to supplement income, Nevin again drove cross-country for a trucking company.

Nevin and Jackie in 2006

Chapter 69

Retirement Years

After 50 years in the pastorate and evangelistic work, God lifted the burden of a pastorate from my husband's heart. Resigning from The Lighthouse Church was "bittersweet," but we knew it was God's Will for our lives. We informed the church Board first, and then made the announcement to the congregation. It came as a shock to many and some wondered why we would resign, but there was no way we could stay when God said, *"GO."*

Our first concern was to find another pastor for the church, so we asked a minister to come to "try out" and he ministered one Sunday morning. We then met with the congregation to see how they felt about him, and they wanted to become better acquainted; therefore, he came back for several Sundays in a row.

There was another congregational meeting, and it did not seem as though it was going to work out because several members said they were going to find another place of worship. We still had a mortgage to pay each month, and with so few members remaining, our only option was to sell the building and pay off the mortgage.

That was not what we wanted, because our desire was to see The Lighthouse Church continue as it had for many more years to come. However, we have learned there is *"a time and a season for all things."* Even though we did not want to admit it, the fact remained that The Lighthouse had finished the work God had planned for it to do.

Across town, there was a small group of Christians meeting in a rented building each weekend, and they were praying that God would provide a church building for them. We were contacted by e-mail and asked to pray for them, and they did not even know about the events that were taking place at The Lighthouse Church.

That morning when I read my e-mails, I saw a name I did not recognize but continued to read the message anyway. I printed it out and showed it to George. It was as though God was telling us that another group of His children needed our building, and even though The Lighthouse would no longer be there, it would still be a church where individuals could come to learn about God's love for mankind.

George called the telephone number provided, and had to leave a message. Pastor Todd Crouch returned the call later. He and some of his members came over to talk to us, and they loved the church. They were so thrilled about the possibility of having their own church building, it reminded me of how exited we were when we bought it years before.

This had to be God's plan, because everything worked out perfectly. They had no trouble in securing the necessary funds, and of course, it took time for all the paperwork to be finished. We decided our last Sunday would be on May 28, 2006, and we had a combined service that day with the Fountain of Life congregation. It was truly a beautiful service, and we were so pleased with the way God had worked everything out for our good and His Glory!

Pastor George and Nadine Van Riper singing at their 50th celebration.

My brother-in-law and sister-in-law, Pastor George and Holly Garancosky, had also moved to Washington and assumed a pastorate at the Abundant Life Baptist Church. It was nice to have them nearby, because Holly was very young when her brother George (my husband) left home to attend Bible school, so they didn't really know each other very well. We have had some very nice times together, and my brother-in-law George, has been a wonderful help to me with the computer. I started using a computer late in life, so I am not very knowledgeable about this new technology. He is such a big help to me when I have a problem I cannot solve, and I appreciate it so very much.

When we retired from The Lighthouse Church, Craig and Melanie decided to become part of The Abundant Life Church family. Craig was always very respectful, and called his pastor Uncle George. They were well received and it was not long until they asked Craig to be their sound engineer. He is a pro in that field and did a great job there. Melanie became a member of the Worship Team and often fills the role of leader.

Chapter 70

Milestone of 50 Years

In the year 2006, we reached a milestone of 50 years faithfully serving God in evangelistic ministry and in the pastorate.

A banquet and concert were held in our honor with 160 people in attendance at the Julian's Banquet Hall in Washington, Pennsylvania.

Our dear friends, Denny and Marge Hazen came from Lewisville, Ohio to act as emcees and were a blessing to everyone. They have a regular telecast in Canton, Ohio of which we had been guests many times over the past 20 years.

Family and friends came from far and near to celebrate with us that evening, and we felt honored they would be a part of this celebration.

Several of our minister friends also attended and we appreciated them taking time from their busy schedules to share in a high point in our lives. We had a blessed evening together and rejoiced in the goodness of our God and Savior.

Several of our music artist friends came and sang a song for us. A special attraction that evening was when The Richter Trio sang a song entitled, "Ode to Old Age." Mikki Richter had written the words concerning how forgetful we can be when we reach our "golden years!" The words were sung to the tune of "Precious Memories," and everyone enjoyed it immensely.

When Mr. Chuck Gratner, his wife Susan, and some staff from WPIT Radio Station in Pittsburgh came forward to present us with a special gift, we were totally surprised.

There were other gifts also, and we appreciated the kindness and generosity of everyone. That evening will be long remembered in our minds and hearts.

This also marked 50 years of my playing instruments in church services, for weddings and funerals, at concerts and special events. It started with an accordion in our early evangelistic years, and then piano, which I had mastered in my youth, and later the organ, which I had the opportunity to learn during a pastorate.

A few years before our retirement, I was invited to play a 20-minute prelude before an Ivan Parker Concert in the Greensburg, Pennsylvania area. It was a joy to play hymns, choruses, and popular gospel songs. Ivan is a guest quite often on the Bill Gaither Videos, and has an awesome singing voice. That was a privilege I thoroughly enjoyed.

Chapter 71

God Is Faithful

Since retiring from The Lighthouse Church, we needed to move our broadcasting studio out of the church building. The Beam of Hope Radio Broadcast is supported by our listing audience, and we felt led to keep the program on the air. It was not feasible to rent a facility for the studio, so we decided to convert one of our bedrooms into a studio and office for George. My office space is in a corner of the dining room.

Occasionally, we pre-record broadcasts, but most of the time we do them live, which seems to be enjoyed by most people. They can call in their prayer requests and we pray during that program, and agree with them that God will hear and answer their prayers.

An incident occurred one Saturday morning that I will never forget! I had been in the studio and came downstairs to take telephone calls. I hung up the telephone after talking with a lady, and all of a sudden I experienced chest pains! This took me by surprise because I had never felt anything like that before in my life. I knew George would want to know what was going on, but I also knew I could not interrupt a live broadcast to tell him I was in pain. So, I placed my hands over my heart and began to pray. I asked God to take the pain away, and Praise God, He did!

On Saturday mornings, we have a three-hour broadcast, so it was noon before I could tell George about the incident. Naturally, he was greatly concerned, but since the pain was gone, we did not go to the Emergency Room. That evening we had planned to go to Scot and Wendy's house for a family cookout. It was very hot and humid that day, and since I was feeling rather tired, we decided to stay home.

Nevin and Jackie were in town and came to visit us in the afternoon. After talking for a while, I told them about the chest pains and they were both very surprised and looked at one another in a knowing glance. They told me later they felt they should move back home to help us. I asked them to please give our apologies to the family, because we just could not join them that evening.

As soon as Nevin told the others, Craig called me right away and said, "Mom, you go to the doctor and find out what is wrong with you, because one of my friends had chest pains and he died." I told him I would check with my doctor the first of the week, because they were not in the office on the weekend.

The next morning, we went to church and as soon as my brother-in-law George saw me, he came right over and said, "Your sons are concerned about you." I said, "I know." He then told me I should go to the doctor, and I assured him I would go the next day. I told my sons I would let them know what the doctor had to say.

So, on Monday, instead of calling the doctor, we drove to his office. We saw one of the nurses and explained the situation. She took us aside and checked the schedule and asked if we could come back at 2:30 p. m. I really appreciated her working me in, because they are extremely busy most of the time.

Doctor Fuerst wanted to know about the pains, so I related the incident to him. He wanted me to have an electrocardiogram, so the nurse took care of that right in the office. It came out fine. The doctor told me the good news was that I had not had a heart attack, but we still didn't know what had caused the pain. I told him I had prayed and God took the pain away. He wanted to be on the safe side and ordered an echocardiogram. That test also came back fine. So, there was no doubt my heart was in good shape! We were so relieved to hear that news! Scot was also concerned and even stopped by our house after work to find out the test results.

The doctor asked about my family history, and of course, I had to tell him my dad died at the age of 52 from a massive heart attack, and my mother died from an aneurysm. My sister and three brothers all had cardiovascular problems, so it seemed to be genetic. He then decided to have blood work done. I had always been healthy and the only surgery I ever had was a cataract removed. I still have my tonsils, and I never had any of these tests taken before. However, I did get a surprise when he called to give me the report.

I had a cholesterol problem. I could hardly believe what the doctor said because I did not have a weight problem and tried to eat nutritional foods for good health. However, when it is genetic, weight is not the issue. I read literature and immediately went on a 95 percent fat-free diet, and let me tell you, that was quite a challenge.

It was well worth the effort, though, because my bad (LDL) cholesterol dropped 48 points in just about ten weeks. However, my good (HDL) cholesterol dropped, too, which was not good. My doctor allowed me to use natural supplements to bring my good cholesterol numbers back up, and with God's help, it will work for me. Of course, I will always watch the fat intake to remain healthy.

About that time, Nevin and Jackie felt a need to move back to Washington to be of help to George and me in our radio ministry. They moved in October of 2007 from their warm Florida climate just in time for cool temperatures in the northeast that precede inevitable winter weather, but it was so nice to have them close by once again.

Nevin has always loved being on the radio, and it was not long until he and Jackie became co-hosts of our daily broadcasts called The Beam of Hope. It was new to Jackie, but she plunged in and learned quickly. She loves it just as much as Nevin. She has a compassionate heart for people and lets them know she truly cares, which is so important in radio ministry.

They worked by our side and were a tremendous help. During broadcasts, we take prayer requests over the telephone and then pray for those requests on the air. There have been many answers to prayer, because faith reached up to our wonderful heavenly father and He responded.

When the radio manager, Chuck Gratner, called and asked if we would like to extend our broadcasting hours, George felt God was giving us an awesome opportunity to spread the "Good News" to a new audience. Of course, without Nevin and Jackie, we could never carry the heavy load, but with their help, could manage nicely.

We had expanded from a half-hour program to a three-hour program six days a week and one hour on Sundays. Our listening audience had the opportunity to share with family and friends that we could be accessed on the Internet through the Pittsburgh radio station's website.

Our financial support comes from our listening audience, and it never ceases to amaze us each month, that because of faithful supporters, all the bills are paid. God is faithful! However, since the program was listener supported, finances were not sufficient to keep Nevin and Jackie with us fulltime. We were disappointed and so were our listeners who called and sent emails with caring messages as our extended family.

Chapter 72

God's Helping Hands

L ife was quite different for us after we retired from the pastorate, and it took me quite a while to adjust to our new schedule. However, we were now free to minister anywhere at any time we were called upon.

One Sunday morning, we were heading to Muncy, Pennsylvania and left early as we planned to attend a church service on the way. We loaded the car and George did not want to get his suit jacket wrinkled, so he hung it in the back seat.

We drove down the steep Old National Pike and took the ramp onto Interstate 70 heading east, and right away we noticed a car pulling up beside us, but not passing us. This seemed strange, but we did not think much about it. Then a man in another car was acting the same way, and still we thought nothing of it. They did not motion to us or try to get our attention—at least, not that we noticed.

After we had driven about ten miles or so, we took an exit to see what might be wrong with our vehicle. To our surprise, both cars also pulled over, and a man jumped out of the first car, paused at the back of our car, and then came to the driver's side window. In his hand was George's wallet, and he told us he didn't want us to lose our money and not ever know it. Then George remembered he had laid his wallet on the trunk of our car when he hung up his jacket, and forgot about it. He does not like to drive with a wallet in his pocket, because it bothers his hip, especially if we are traveling for a few hours. The man in the second car apparently saw everything was under control, so he turned and went on his way. It had to be the Hand of God that held that wallet on our trunk, because later on, we laid it back down on the trunk, and gave it a little push, and it fell right off!

We told the man how grateful we were for his kindness and then we praised God for His goodness. George had put some extra cash in his wallet that morning, because the next day we planned to stop at a tool shop where he wanted to make some purchases. God is so good and is looking out for us, even when we don't realize it!

Chapter 73

Losing A Brother

Once again the Holiday Season was drawing near, and it would soon be time to celebrate the Birth of our Savior, Jesus Christ. That is always a wonderful occasion, because without Jesus' birth, death and resurrection, we would not have the opportunity to spend eternity in heaven.

The year 2007 was coming to a close, and it was hard to believe another year had come and gone. It seems like the older I get the faster time goes by! However, the year would not end without heartache.

It was very early in the morning on December 8 when we awoke to the telephone ringing, and at that hour, the news is usually not good. I answered and it was my niece, Tammy, who lives in Mifflinburg, Pennsylvania. She was crying as she told me that her dad, who was my youngest brother (Junior), had passed away. It came as a shock to everyone, including me.

She explained that he had gotten up about 5:30 a.m. and went to the bathroom, and then went back to bed; however, a few minutes later, took his last breath. Why the Lord took him so suddenly we do not understand, but none of us know when our time will come so it pays to be ready to meet our maker.

Junior had suffered a stroke about 16 years earlier, and his right side was totally paralyzed. He had been faithful to do the prescribed exercises, and with God's help was doing very well. He could not drive anymore, but did manage to drive their riding mower to cut grass.

He was very limited in his abilities and would not be defeated. He even sat on the ground to plant flowers in front of their house every year. They were so beautiful that a local newspaper reporter stopped by and took pictures, and an article showed up on the front page. People would also drive by just to see the gorgeous array of flowers that lined their corner property. They always seemed to be picture perfect!

My sister-in-law, Rhoda, wanted George to conduct the funeral service. She also asked if we would sing a song, and of course, we were happy to help in any way we could.

It is wonderful to know he is in heaven and we will see him again some day; however, he is greatly missed by family and friends. We were so glad Nevin and Jackie could make the trip with us because it also gave Nevin an opportunity to reconnect with some of his distant family. Unfortunately, it often takes the loss of a loved one for those left behind to better appreciate the importance of close family ties.

I also read a poem entitled, "Christmas In Heaven," which was comforting to the family, but also brought tears to our eyes. Here is that poem with my brother's name inserted in parentheses as I read it at the funeral.

Christmas In Heaven

I see the countless Christmas Trees around the world below,
With tiny lights like heaven's stars, reflecting on the snow.
The sight is so spectacular; please wipe away that tear,
For I am (Junior is) spending Christmas with Jesus Christ this
year.
I hear the many Christmas songs that people hold so dear,
But the sound of music cannot compare with the Christmas
choir up here.
I have no words to tell you the joy their voices bring,
For it is beyond description to hear the angels sing.
I know how much you miss me; I see the pain inside your heart,
But I am not so far away, we really aren't apart.
So be happy for me dear ones, you know I hold you dear.
I send you each a memory of my undying love.
After all, love is a gift more precious than pure gold.
It is always most important in the stories Jesus told.
Please love each other as the Father said to do,
For I cannot count the blessings or love He has for you.
So have a Merry Christmas and wipe away that tear and remember
I am (Junior is) spending Christmas with Jesus Christ this year.

— Author Unknown

Everyone is usually really busy during the Holiday Season, until after New Year's Eve, and then things slow down a bit. George felt in his heart that we should get our family together, especially our three sons and their wives. The feeling was so urgent that we planned it for New Year's Day, which seemed like the opportune time. We called our three sons and also George and Holly, and invited all of them to our house. I prepared dinner and we had a wonderful time around the table.

George felt we should pray a special blessing upon their lives, so when the meal was over, we gathered in the living room. George and I laid our hands on Nevin and Jackie, then on Craig and Melanie, and then on Scot and Wendy and asked God to bless them in a special way and to keep His hand upon their lives and to use them for His glory! We also prayed for George and Holly, and then the family prayed for us. It truly was a wonderful time of prayer together.

The following Sunday, Craig told his pastor (his Uncle George) how much he appreciated the prayer time on New Year's Day. Little did any of us know what we would have to face the very next week.

Chapter 74

Sorrow Of The Heart

During our many years of ministry, we had comforted numerous individuals as they suffered heartache and pain, especially in the loss of loved ones. Some had been small children, some middle age and others elderly. It is never easy to lose someone you love and hold dear to your heart. We had never dreamed we would be the ones needing comfort and sympathy, until January 7, 2008. When I first started to write this book, I never imagined I would be including this chapter, but now I must, because it is an experience that will stay with me for the rest of my life!

Since we had retired from the pastorate and moved our radio studio and offices to our home, it seemed we were always at work. We should have been able to relax more, but if there was work waiting to be done at the end of the day, it seemed there was always a magnet drawing me back to my desk. Therefore, about three or four times a year, we would pack a suitcase and take a trip somewhere. After two or three days, we were ready to go back to work, and it was always good to get home again.

In Pennsylvania, January is usually very cold with a blanket of snow covering the ground most of the time, but 2008 was different. The temperature reached the high 60s for several days that first week. So, we thought it would be a great time to head to one of our favorite places, Pigeon Forge, Tennessee. We always enjoyed going when it was "off season," which meant it would be very quiet and there would be very few vacationers there. It was much easier to relax without the hustle and bustle of a crowd.

One place we always enjoyed visiting was called Cades Cove. It was about 20 miles from Pigeon Forge. Once we reached the cove, there was a one-way lane that took us out into the country where old homesteads were located but had been vacated many years before. There were also some very old churches along the way, and the doors were always open. If anyone wanted to go in for a while, they could, and one time we did stop and go inside. There were several folks there, and we sang some songs together, and had a nice time. It took us about 30 to 45 minutes to drive those 11 miles, but it was always very enjoyable and relaxing.

It was not unusual to see deer right along the road, and some folks had even seen a bear or two on occasion. However, we had never been fortunate enough to see a bear in that area, but did see one as we rode along a country road about an hour from home one day. We had just crossed a mountain near our home and were coming down the other side when a bear walked out of the woods. It had the most beautiful black lustrous coat, and we slowed down to get a better look. Of course, the bear turned and headed back toward the woods, so we continued down the hill. I looked back just as it lumbered across the road behind us.

So, on that Saturday evening in January, we made some last minute plans to take a few days off. We were up early on Sunday morning, dressed for church, and put our luggage in the car. We had enough time to drive to Weston, West Virginia for the morning worship service at a church that had been our pastorate 50 years before. That's where we lived when our middle son, Craig, was born.

We enjoyed the service and afterward ate lunch, and then continued on our way. The trip was very enjoyable, and after several hours we reached our destination. We had called ahead to reserve our lodging, and arrived there in the evening. After a very relaxing time and a good night's rest, we went out to see the sights. We enjoyed looking in some of the shops. I enjoy dress shops and George enjoys the tool shops.

We had planned to drive to Cades Cove later that day, but when evening came, we decided to stay in and relax, and go the next day. It was about 7:30 when our cell phone rang, and I answered it. I saw it was Nevin, and it was never unusual for him to call us, no matter where we were.

When I answered, he was crying but managed to say, "Mom, I hate to have to tell you this, but Craig had an accident on his motorcycle and he's gone." I said, "Craig's gone. Oh, no!" George could see the shocked look on my face, so I handed the telephone to him, and buried my face in my hands and sobbed aloud. It seemed almost impossible to believe that my son was dead; one whom I had carried inside me for nine months, had given birth to, and cuddled in my arms as an infant; one that I had nurtured and cared for all those years. Could this really be true? Would I wake up and find it had all been a bad dream? Unfortunately, that was not the case.

After George talked with Nevin, we embraced each other and cried and prayed. We then called a few of our friends and family, and asked them to please remember our family in prayer as we dealt with this terrible tragedy. Our sons also called other family and close friends. It was unbelievable that we would never see him walk through our kitchen door again with that huge smile and those beautiful big brown eyes. He had his own construction business, and quite often in the evening, would stop by to sit and chat with us for a while.

It would have been impossible to sleep that night, so we packed up our things and headed for home. Nevin called back and offered to meet us half way so we would not be alone for that eight-hour trip. He and Jackie met us in Beckley, West Virginia. Nevin drove our car with his dad, and I rode with Jackie.

It was about 4:30 a.m. when we arrived home, and we were extremely exhausted. The trauma of the accident had completely drained our strength. After unloading the car, we went to bed and tried to sleep. I think we may have slept about two hours, and then we arose, tried to eat breakfast, had devotions, and did a live radio broadcast of The Beam of Hope from 9 to 9:30 a.m. We had been broadcasting for years, and our radio audience had become family to us; therefore, we wanted to tell them what had happened. Nevin and Jackie joined us, and through our tears, managed to tell our audience about Craig's accident.

Craig had finished a construction job and planned to go to 84 Lumber in Bridgeville to get directions for a job site the next day. It was so warm he decided to ride the bike, because he had very little time for pleasure riding. He left his house and five minutes later, rode down the ramp onto Interstate 70, heading east. He passed a car, and when he pulled back into the right lane, his bike began to shake. A witness said it looked like he was getting it under control when it started shaking violently and threw him off. At that time, he was crossing a bridge and was thrown against the concrete and died instantly.

Craig had been a biker for years and traveled thousands of miles without an accident, and this did not seem possible, so we were wondering what could have happened. The autopsy showed Craig was fine, so we assumed something had gone wrong with the bike, but we do not know for sure. Maybe we will never know!

Many of our radio broadcast listeners had met Craig, because he and Melanie went with us when we ministered in other churches, at banquets, and at our annual Jubilee Celebration Concerts. Craig was our Sound Engineer and Melanie sang with us. Everyone was just as shocked as we were to hear the news, and the outpouring of love and sympathy that was shown to us during our time of sorrow deeply touched our hearts.

Melanie was at work when the accident happened. So, a police officer was dispatched to inform her of this tragedy, along with the coroner. Another state trooper, who happened to be a friend of Craig's, knew she worked at JC Penney and joined them.

Melanie was told the store's head manager wanted to see her in the office and she wondered why. Going back the hallway, she passed a security guard who assured her she was not in trouble. When she stepped into the office and saw the officers standing with a man in a suit, her heart began to pound. The man in the suit was a coroner and he spoke to Melanie, saying he had to tell her about an accident that day and confirmed that Craig was her husband, additionally asking her to confirm his driver's license I.D.

She had no idea Craig had ridden his bike that afternoon and the coroner explained that the accident had been pretty bad. While she was thinking she would have to leave work to go to the hospital, the coroner was saying that the accident was really bad and that Craig had actually died.

Denial set in quickly and Melanie kept saying, "This can't be true." She hoped and believed that when she returned home, she would see Craig's motorcycle in the garage, call the family, and let them know it was not true. Unless you have experienced this kind of shock and pain of losing a life partner, one cannot comprehend how terribly difficult it was for her to receive such devastating news.

It appeared she was in shock or denial when her mother came to pick her up. She kept thinking it had to be a mistake. When she arrived at home, she hurried to the garage because she knew that if Craig's motorcycle was there, it could not have been him in that accident, and that he was alright. When she saw the bike was gone, that was the moment she realized she had to face reality and would not see him again in this life. She felt such tremendous loss, and the pain and sorrow were overwhelming.

Even though she knew she would see him again in heaven, that did not stop the tears from flowing or tremendous sadness in her heart. It would take months or maybe even years for the grief to subside, and she would miss him for the rest of her life.

She called her two daughters. Mandy, who lived nearby, came to her side as quickly as possible. Her oldest daughter, Celina, was living in Denver, Colorado, and had just flown to California on business. As soon as she got the message, she immediately purchased a ticket for a flight back to Denver and packed another bag before flying to Pittsburgh. She arrived the very next day.

It was a very difficult time for all of us, and especially when we went to make the arrangements for the funeral. We were told we should come to view the body before the 2 p.m. public viewing and should decide if we wanted the public to view him or not. Actually, we were amazed at how natural he looked, having had such a terrible accident.

The viewing was scheduled for 2 to 4 and 7 to 9 p.m. on Thursday, January 10, at Neal's Funeral Home on Allison Avenue in Washington, Pennsylvania. We arrived at 1 p.m. on Thursday, and shortly after 1:30 the Funeral Home became filled with friends and loved ones wanting to pay their respects. There was a continuous line until about 5 p.m., at which time we all took a short break to get a bite to eat. By 6 p.m., the building filled up once again, and we did not leave until 11 o'clock that night. We were told there were approximately 1,000 people that came, and that it was the second largest viewing they had ever had.

We were deeply touched by so many town officials that came, including Judge Mark Mascara, Commissioners Diana Irey and Larry Maggi. The radio station manager who is also our personal friend, Mr. Chuck Gratner and his wife Susan, came and several other staff members as well. The manager of Community Bank, Lisa, and other bank officials came, plus our dentist, Doctor Kring, and his staff stopped by after work. Also, many of our ministerial friends came, and many individuals waited in line 2 to 3 hours on that rainy day. There were many others too numerous to mention, and we appreciated each one so very much. We learned later on that other people came, but could not find a place to park, so they had to leave without paying their respects.

On Friday, another viewing began at 11 a.m. in The Abundant Life Baptist Church where the funeral was held at 1 p.m. The church was filled and our brother-in-law, Pastor George Garancosky officiated. I must say here that Craig was not a minister and did not preach to people; however, they saw something in his life that assured them he was a born-again Christian, and the love of Jesus shone through his life.

The pastor asked if anyone would like to say a few words about Craig, and there were several individuals that made comments concerning how Craig's life had made an impact on them.

Celina and Mandy made some wonderful comments about their dad, and John told what a great father-in-law Craig was to him and that he had taught him many things.

Nevin and Scot described what Craig's life meant to them as a brother highlighting the closeness between the brothers blended with a bit of typical Van Riper humor that helped ease some tension many were dealing with during the service.

I then took a moment and related an incident that had happened to Craig in Georgia. Craig had drifted from God and started drinking and running with the wrong crowd. One night while intoxicated, he started to drive home, which was a big mistake. He was in a rural area and passed out behind the wheel. Something jarred him awake and he grabbed onto the steering wheel just as the car plunged down an incline flipping end to end until it crashed at the bottom. It was a miracle he was not killed then from a severe head injury and we thanked God he did not bleed to death before arriving at the hospital. He was still conscious and coherent and managed to crawl up to the road in the wee hours of that morning in time to see a car pass by. It stopped and backed up.

Craig's blood was flowing down his face and onto his clothing, but the female driver helped him into her car and rushed him to the emergency room. All the while, my son was more concerned about getting blood on the car's white interior. After dropping him off, she went on her way. It took 19 staples to close his wound, which was a big gash from ear to ear. To this day, none of us know who that driver was or where she came from; however, I still believe she was an angel sent from God to save Craig's life.

As parents, we always pray for God's protection for our children and grandchildren, and most of all for their salvation. If Craig had died in that crash, we would never see him again. But, now I know I will see him in heaven, because he had invited Christ back into his heart, and God had turned his life around. We are so blessed!

Melanie asked us to sing if we felt we could, and I thank God that He enabled us to do so. We sang the song, entitled "I Won't Have To Worry Anymore," and mentioned Craig by name in the song. She also requested that our good friends, Gary and MarJean Miller, also known as "Promise," sing "If You Could See Where I Am, You Wouldn't Cry." The song was very meaningful that day, but it was difficult to hold back tears. We all knew Craig was in a much better place where there would be no more pain or sorrow, but we will miss him until we go to be with him in heaven some day. Things would never be the same again, and we had to learn to adjust to a different way of life.

That week was a very difficult one for me, and I had no desire to eat; however, I forced myself to consume a little bit of food each day, so I could keep going. I lost about six pounds and could feel depression trying to take hold of my life. The enemy of my soul tried his best to defeat me, but knowing it would only make things worse, I fought against it, and God gave me the victory!

Of course, it is not easy for us when we get together as a family, knowing that one is missing! I know we are not the only ones to have lost a loved one, but I must admit that until this point in our lives, we did not fully comprehend the traumatic feeling of pain and grief that comes with the loss of a child. We brought three boys into this world, and we thank God for each one, and even though Craig left us early, we are thankful for the 49 years God allowed him to be with us. Between our three sons and their wives, we have been blessed with three granddaughters and four grandsons, all of whom are very intelligent and talented. There is an age-old saying that when a loved one passes on, there is a new birth in the family. It was not long after when Lindsey gave birth to our great-granddaughter. We love each and every one.

A few weeks after the funeral, George had retired for the evening, but in the early morning hours was awakened from his sleep. He felt compelled to get up and go to the computer and here is what he wrote.

"WILL THE TEARS EVER STOP?"

On Monday, January 7, 2008 at 4:07 p.m., the unthinkable and most devastating incident happened to our family. Nadine and I were taking a few days of R & R in Pigeon Forge, Tennessee. We were watching a program on television, when our cell phone rang, about 7:30 p.m. Nadine answered the phone and I noticed the shocked look on her face, and heard her cry out, "Oh, no!" She handed me the phone, and then began to weep, and now many weeks later, the tears are still falling. As I talked with Nevin, he told me that our middle son, Craig, had been killed in a motorcycle accident. Now, the tears began to roll down my face and they are still rolling.

Tears are a language that God understands, so the songwriter puts it. The scripture tells us that Jesus wept at the tomb of Lazarus, and He also wept over Jerusalem. There is another song that says ten thousand angels cried. I believe that God, our Heavenly Father, does understand the sorrow that comes into our lives in many different ways. Divorce, incurable diseases, miscarriages, loved ones killed in battle and many other hurtful conditions may cross our pathway. Why does a Loving Heavenly Father allow such things?

If God is God, and can roll back the sea, can create the worlds with His Word, keep the planets in orbit, why would He allow such hurtful situations to come into our lives if He loves us? Why would He allow our eyes to run like rivers, with seemingly no end? I wish I had the answer, but I don't. However, I do know that He loves us and He demonstrated that love by giving His Only Begotten Son, Jesus Christ, to die for us, so that we could have eternal life. God does not necessarily allow bad things to happen to good people, but when they do, He is always there to pick us up and soothe our hurts.

I can testify to the fact that, when we received the news of Craig's death, the peace of God that passeth all understanding began to fill my heart and soul, and it does keep me in those devastating times. There was a time several years ago, when things went wrong in my ministry and in my family. I got really mad at God, because

I felt that He was very unfair. Nadine and I had served Him to the best of our ability and still things were going from bad to worse. I am deeply sorry to this day that I got bitter instead of leaning on the Grace and Peace of God at that time.

Now, faced with the greatest of tragedy in any parent's life, the loss of a child, His peace was filling my soul. Did I feel hurt? Oh yes, and it was deeper than I ever thought possible. Do I have questions? Yes, by the dozen. Do I weep when I hear Craig's voice on his answering machine? Yes. Will I ever get over this tragedy? I doubt it! However, I do know the God that we serve and love will comfort our hearts from now, until we see *Jesus,* and meet Craig in Heaven.

Thank God, when we know Christ as our Savior, death is not the end of the story. As Paul Harvey has stated so many times, "and now for the rest of the story." Craig loved the Lord and was a vital part of our lives for 49 years. We can say the time was short, or that is a young age to be killed, but we can also say, "Thank God for 49 years!"

Craig's life had some rough places in it, but through it all, God turned him around and he served the Lord without compromise. He was greatly loved by many and the fact that over 1,000 came to his viewing certainly was a testimony to his life. We are hearing many wonderful reports of how he touched so many lives. It makes our hearts proud to be his parents.

Craig served as our sound engineer when we would go out in concerts. He also was ever ready to help his mom and dad, whenever we needed him. We won't see him walk through the door again, and come in to visit with us, as he would do from time to time in the evening. But, someday he will welcome us home in heaven, when our time comes to go.

Will the tears ever stop??? I doubt it, because tears sometimes come from memory, and we will always have memories. What can we do when grief and sorrow seems overwhelming? We can run to the Father, who also lost a Son at Calvary, and He will give us comfort and peace. We will constantly and daily need to rest in His love.

Will the tears ever stop? Probably not! A picture, a song, a touch, a letter, a telephone call, or a particular place will bring a flood of memories and a river of tears. But, remember, tears and laughter are two emotions that God has given us to save us from total collapse or a nervous breakdown. It is in times like these, that we must draw from the faith in our hearts, "That God doeth all things well." At your weakest point, God will bring someone or something into your life that will lift you and sustain you. How He does it, I don't know, but I do know, "He Does It!" My life and my family can testify to that fact.

When we heard of Craig's untimely death, the hurt was deep. We had never experienced grief or inner pain like this. The sorrow of heart was so deep that it seemed like I was walking through a dark valley and did not know the way out. My heart cried out, "Oh, God please help me. It is dark all around me, but please Lord, just take my hand and walk me through this valley." I can truly say, He has done that very thing for me.

We will always miss Craig's laughter and kindness, but faith tells us that we shall see him again. This is not the final page to the story. Our hope is in the scripture, "We shall all be changed, in the twinkling of an eye, and we shall be with Jesus and our loved one!" There will be no more dying, no more sickness, no more parting and NO MORE TEARS! Our journey will be complete, when we see Jesus.

Craig Van Riper
1958 - 2008

Chapter 75

Life Without Craig

John and Mandy lived in an apartment in Eighty Four, Pennsylvania, but immediately went to be with Melanie. They knew how difficult it would be for her to be alone at such a traumatic time. Melanie told them she would love for them to move in with her, so they did.

A couple weeks passed and one Sunday morning, Melanie had already gone to church and Mandy was looking for clothes to wear when the telephone rang. When she answered, the lady on the other end asked, *"Hello, is Craig there?"* to which, Mandy hesitantly said, *"No."* The lady then responded with *"Has he gone to church?"* *"No, he hasn't,"* Mandy replied, and then added, *"I guess you haven't heard about his accident."* The lady said, *"No, I haven't."* She explained to the lady that Craig had been tragically killed. The lady then began to cry, and said how sorry she was to hear the news. She also said the Van Riper family had been on her heart, and she wanted to call to see how everyone was doing. She told Mandy that Craig had done some repair work for her mother and was such a nice young man. He had also mentioned about the church he attended and invited the family to the services.

Craig's Christian testimony will live on and on because he always let his light shine for Jesus, no matter where he was or whom he was with. Other contractors and clerks at the lumberyards noticed Craig never swore or used bad language, and was honest to a fault. In fact, there was one lumberyard where he purchased most of his supplies, and they would allow him to go to the yard and pick out the lumber he wanted. He told them what he had selected and they knew they could trust him to tell the truth. He has been gone from us for some time now, but we are still hearing about the wonderful and thoughtful deeds he did for others who were in need.

A number of individuals have assured us that our lives would get back to normal some day. However, Nevin mentioned the fact that our lives would never be *"normal"* again, because our *"normal"* included Craig. He would never attend another family reunion or any other family get-together, nor would he go with us to another concert, or church service, and that broke our hearts! There will always be things that will remind us of Craig, and the tears will flow again and again.

Of course, when we think of Craig now, we can picture him in heaven, rejoicing and praising God that he is in his new home that was prepared for him. Those of us that are left behind are the ones that grieve and miss him so very much; however, we know that one day we will be reunited with him in heaven when Jesus calls us home. That is one reunion we do not want to miss!

Chapter 76

Highlight Of My Golden Years

Winter finally faded into the background, and spring once again made its appearance. Warm days are always so inviting, and it is wonderful to be able to sit out on the porch again and feel a warm light wind blowing.

George asked me what I would like to do for my birthday, which was fast approaching. I heard "Dino" was going to be in concert in Canton, Ohio on April 4, which was one day after my birthday. Dino Kartsonakis is known as America's piano showman whom I call a genius on the keyboard. So, I told George I would love to go to that concert. We called for tickets and made our plans to attend, and it was a wonderful concert as he is one of the finest pianists I know.

We had great seats, just about 6 rows from the stage right in the center section. After about 30 minutes of tremendous music, Dino and Cheryl told us they were grandparents. Then he asked how many grandmothers were in the audience, and of course, I raised my hand.

His next question was, "How many of you play the piano?" I was not going to raise my hand, but George told me to, so I did. Dino looked at me and told me to stand up. He then asked how many years I had been playing, to which I responded, "About 60 years." He put his hands on his hips and said, "Well, you should be good!" I did not respond to that, and then he asked if I could play by ear, and I told him, "Yes."

Then a lady in front of me had her hand raised, and he asked how long she had been playing to which she responded 49 years. He then told me to sit down, which I did. Then he asked the other lady if she could play by ear, to which she responded, "No, I need the music." He then told her to sit down, and told me to stand up again, and called me to the stage. He met me at the stairs, took my hand, and led me to center stage.

We talked a little bit, and then he told me we were going to play a duet together on the piano. In fact, he told me we were going to play three songs, and asked if I knew the song, "Put A Nickel In It," to which I responded, "No, I don't know that one." He then asked if I knew, "Twelfth Street Rag." I looked at him and said, "I play in church, Dino," and everybody laughed out loud, including him.

Then he wanted to know if I could play "When the Saints Go Marching In," and I told him I knew that one! He told me to sit down and play it for him, which I did. After that, he sat down also, and we played together for several minutes. It was so exciting, and I was so nervous, but I enjoyed it immensely! In fact, it was the "Highlight of my Golden Years!" George later told me the audience gave me a standing ovation when I played alone, and then another one after we played our duet, but I didn't even notice.

Dino Kartsonakis, America's piano showman,
takes Nadine by the hand and talks about songs
they were going to play as a duet in front of a full house
during a concert in Canton, Ohio.

Afterward, Dino told me he wanted to give me something, and asked if I had noticed the locket that Cheryl was wearing. I told him it was beautiful, and he handed me a jewelry box. Inside was a locket exactly like hers! I asked if I could give him a hug and thanked him for such a lovely gift. He certainly is a gentleman and is very kind and thoughtful. That is one evening I will never forget.

By now, you are thinking George planned all this in advance in recognition of my birthday. Right? Well, he didn't. In fact, several people approached me afterward and inquired if I was a plant in the audience. I wasn't, but it was amusing that they thought so. The experience was truly memorable.

Dino and Cheryl have an annual Christmas Show in Branson, Missouri for a whole month, and it must be spectacular, because I believe the auditorium is filled night after night. I would love to go there and see that show sometime.

Chapter 77

Reflection

As I look back on the first few years of my life, I can see where God had a plan, and Satan tried to destroy it. It ranged from a serious childhood illness at only six weeks of age to childhood accidents that could have taken my life. Each time, I was spared.

The first incident occurred just shortly after I was born. Childhood diseases were prevalent, and when the whooping cough came our way, it hit me with full force. There were times I coughed so hard, I could hardly get my breath. My family spent hours caring for me, and trying to help me through this terrible ordeal. There were times when my parents thought for sure they would lose their little baby who had been with them just six short weeks, because my tiny body just didn't have the strength it needed to fight back. Satan tried to take my life, *but God had another plan!*

The second dealt with matches. Many children are intrigued watching a flame come to life from a match head, and my youngest brother was no exception. Junior was playing with matches one day, and I couldn't help but get closer for a better look. In the process, though, my skirt caught on fire. I thank the Lord to this day for His helping hand and Junior's swift response to smother the fire before it engulfed my body. My clothing was singed, but we both were safe. *I know that God had another plan!*

Nadine and her youngest brother Junior

At about two years of age, I loved riding in a little kiddie car. These were not like the plastic ones made today with little engines in them to simulate a real car. It had four wheels but was powered by my little feet. While playing in it on our porch one day, I ventured too close to the edge and the little car with me still inside plunged to the ground. My bottom teeth cut through the skin below my lower lip. I could have been seriously injured or even suffered a broken neck during this traumatic accident, but looking back on it, I believe all things have a certain outcome according to God's plan. Panicked parents run to the rescue of their children, but my future was already laid out and God kept me safe that day *according to His plan.*

Like George, I also experienced a near drowning incident. At about ten years of age, I joined friends at a lake but was afraid of water and could not swim. Venturing out too far, I got into a situation where I could have drowned but someone pulled me to safety. To this day, I don't know who saved me, but I do know that *God had another plan for my life!*

In later years, George met Ron Morehart shortly after he became a Christian and they became good friends. As years passed by, Ron married Gail and eventually they moved to Clarksville, Virginia. His home business sharpening saw blades for gigantic lumber mills in that area grew rapidly, and he began to construct a new spacious building a few miles from his house.

Knowing George was an excellent carpenter, he called to see if he would lend a hand for a few days. We packed a couple suitcases and made the trip to their home where we stayed while George assisted Ron. I usually went with him to work and helped as needed.

One day, I went to purchase some sodas for us, and upon returning looked around but found no place to set them down. Without thinking of the danger, I saw the little ledge on the bottom of the open three-phase breaker box, and put one of the cans on it. As I set the can down and before I could release it, the can leaned inward and touched one of the hot poles, which caused me to become grounded. Immediately, the current burned a hole through that can, and the soda drained to the floor. I was knocked backwards, but was able to keep from falling. A bruise three inches in diameter instantly appeared black and blue on my wrist, which was broken blood vessels caused by the electric current passing through my body. I could have been electrocuted that day but once again, God had spared my life!

Reflecting back over the years of our ministry, it is evident the Hand of God was with us, provided for our needs sometimes even before we began to pray for resolution, and gave us safety over the years as we followed God's Will. Above all, we were the vessels to lead others to the throne. We all have trials and tribulations to overcome, and I hope this book has been an inspiration to you in some way.

Even though we lived from paycheck to paycheck at times and endured some hardships, we stayed focused on the Word. There were times our home was broken into, itself a traumatic experience, and we were alarmed when awakened one night with thrashing noises in the basement that turned out to be a curious critter that found its way inside, a roach infestation at one of our overnight accommodations, and a number of breakdowns of our well-used vehicles and individuals God sent our way to provide assistance. God Bless them for answering His call when it came!

If you are ever in doubt that God has a plan for your life, please doubt no more! Because He does, and when you don't know which way to turn, just ask God for guidance. Then stand back and watch Him work, because He likes to work when nothing else will! He will open doors for you that He wants you to walk through. You will make mistakes, because being human, we all do, but God is always there to help you get back on the right track. There are times when it is not easy to follow God's leading, but if you truly want to obey God, He will always give you the strength and the where-with-all to do it!

God is faithful.

and

GOD HAS A PLAN FOR YOUR LIFE!

Rev. George E. Van Riper, III was ordained as a minister in 1958. He grew up in Pennsylvania and enjoyed growing vegetables and raising animals believing all the while that he was destined to be a career farmer. However, after accepting Christ as his Savior in his teens, he felt in his heart that his life's calling would be in the ministry. He studied diligently to become a vessel God could use, and proved he would stay true to his calling, even during the hardest of times in his life.

Nadine Van Riper is an accomplished pianist and organist. She was born and raised in West Virginia with music a great part of her life and her family's life. It was not until the family moved to Pennsylvania and she met George that she knew she would become a minister's wife. She trusted God throughout the years and held onto her faith during some of the most devastating trials anyone would ever have to face. God has never let her down and she knows He never will.

Since George was ordained, the couple has hosted a live radio program sharing their own professionally recorded southern gospel style music along with prayer and praise reports with their listening audience. They have also appeared on television and hold concerts.

If you have been blessed by God's messages in this book, we would appreciate hearing from you. Please write to us at:

Pastor George and Nadine Van Riper
P.O. Box 122
Washington, PA 15301-0122

Visit our website www.beamofhoperadio.com for more information and to view the calendar of events.

Send email to beamofhope@comcast.net or call 724-228-2008 between the hours of 9 a.m. and 5 p.m. eastern time Monday through Saturday.

Listen to The Beam Of Hope Broadcast on the Internet at the 73 WPIT-AM website www.wpitam.com at 9 a.m. Monday through Saturday, and Sunday at 7:30 a.m. and click on the link to listen live.